2004 EDITION

Greenberg's
GUIDES

AMERICAN FLYER®

AND OTHER S GAUGE MANUFACTURERS
POCKET PRICE GUIDE

Editor: Kent J. Johnson
with assistance from Roger Carp

D1706442

KALMBACH
BOOKS

Twentieth Edition

For more information, visit our website at
www.kalmbachbooks.com
Manufactured in the United States of America

We are constantly striving to improve *Greenberg's Pocket Price Guides*. If you find any missing items or detect any misinformation, please, by all means, write to us. If you have any recommendations for improving a listing, we would like to hear from you. Send your comments, new information, or corrections to:

Editor—American Flyer Pocket Guide (10-8604)
Books Division
Kalmbach Publishing Co.
21027 Crossroads Circle
P.O. Box 1612
Waukesha, WI 53187-1612

Or via e-mail: books@kalmbach.com

Lionel and American Flyer are the registered trademarks of Lionel LLC, Chesterfield, Michigan

Cover design: Kristi Ludwig
Book layout: Julia Gerlach

Cover photo: Provided by John Heck, no. (210)88 F.Y.&P. 4-4-0 steam locomotive produced between 1959 and 1960 by A.C. Gilbert Company.

CONTENTS

INTRODUCTION 4
    What Products Are Listed 4
    How Products Are Listed 4
    How Product Values Are Listed 4
    How Product Values Are Determined 5
    How to Read This Guide 6

TOY TRAIN COLLECTING 8

ANNUAL MARKET REPORT 10
    CTT Market Basket Recap 10
    The S Gauge Marketplace 12

SECTION 1: Gilbert Production 1946-1966 13

SECTION 2: Lionel Production 1979-2004 39

SECTION 3: American Models 1981-2004 49

SECTION 4: S-Helper Service 1994-2004 69

SECTION 5: Gilbert Catalogs & Paper 1946-1966 . . . 90

ABBREVIATIONS 95

What Products Are Listed

This Pocket Price Guide lists the full array of toy train products built by the A.C. Gilbert Company, Lionel Trains, Inc. or Lionel, LLC. This list of items also includes ready-to-run items from two contemporary S Gauge manufacturers, American Models and S-Helper Service. This list of items also includes some products tentatively planned for production in 2004, but not yet released at the time of publication. Subsequent additions and deletions to the 2004 product line will be reported in the next edition of this pocket guide.

How Products Are Listed

This guide is divided into four major sections, each representing a significant type of production: Gilbert, Lionel, American Models, and S-Helper Service.

In the first four sections, production is listed **numerically**, using the item's catalog number. In some cases, manufacturers numbered products with a number different from the catalog number. In these cases we also list this number, enclosed in parentheses, and refer the reader to the published catalog number for the full product description.

Dates cited in this guide are cataloged dates. If there is no catalog date, production dates are listed, if known. While many products are frequently marked with "Built" or "New" dates, these dates may or may not have any relation to catalog dates or actual production dates.

How Product Values Are Listed

We have provided three columns for items listed in Sections 1 through 4. The first two columns give the current market values for each piece. In the Gilbert section, values are denoted for items in Good and Excellent condition. In the Lionel section, values are given for items in New condition. In the American Models and S-Helper Service sections, values reflect the manufacturers' suggested retail price (MSRP) at the time the item was first issued. The "Cond/$" column is for noting the condition and cost of items you acquire.

How Product Values Are Determined

The values presented in this Pocket Price Guide are meant to serve only as a guide to collectors. They are an averaged reflection of prices for items bought and sold across the country, and are intended to assist the collector in making informed decisions concerning purchases and sales.

Values listed herein are based on values obtained at train meets held throughout the nation during the Spring and Summer of 2003, and from private transactions reported by members of our nationwide review panel. Values in your area may be consistent with values published in this guide, or higher or lower, depending upon the relative availability, scarcity, or desirability of a particular item. General economic conditions in your area may also affect values. Even regional preferences for specific roadnames may be a factor.

If you are selling a train to an individual who is planning to resell it—a retailer, for example—you will NOT obtain the values reported in this book. Rather, you may expect to receive about 50 percent of these prices. For your item to be of interest to such a buyer, it must be purchased for considerably less than the price listed here. But if you are dealing one-to-one with another private collector, values may be expected to be more consistent with this guide.

Our studies of train values indicate that mail order and retail store prices are generally higher than prices found at train meets because of the cost and effort of running a retail establishment or producing and distributing a price list, as well as packing and shipping trains.

The values quoted in this guide are for the most common variety of each item. Some rare variations are worth considerably more, and a few of the more significant ones are cited. For more detailed information about variations, please refer to our comprehensive line of collector guides.

Note that new products usually enter the list at their suggested retail price, since most have yet to sell regularly on the secondary market.

WE STRONGLY RECOMMEND THAT NOVICE COLLECTORS SEEK THE ADVICE AND ASSISTANCE OF FRIENDS OR ASSOCIATES WHO HAVE EXPERIENCE IN BUYING, SELLING, AND TRADING TRAINS.

How to Read This Guide

PRODUCT NUMBER
- **(#)** Numbers that have been put in parentheses by us do not appear on the actual items.
- **[#]** means decorations which make this item unique were not done by Lionel.
- **No Number** means item may have lettering, but lacks an item number.
- **(no letters)** means no lettering or number appears on the item.
- ***** means excellent reproductions have been made.

24109   C & O Gondola, *57-60*
            (A) Silver plastic cardboard pi|
            (B) Brown plastic pipes
            (C) Orange cardboard pipes
24110   Pennsylvania Gondola, *59u*
(24112)   See 916
24113   Delaware & Hudson Gondola,

DESCRIPTION
The text description for most items identifies the road (railroad) name, equipment type, equipment number (indicated in quotes), notable color or lettering data, and the year the item was first cataloged or produced (those dates followed by a "u" denote uncataloged items).

CONDITION

Trains and related items are usually classified by condition relating to appearance. The following definitions apply for this guide:

- **FAIR**—well-scratched, chipped, dented, rusted, or warped condition.
- **GOOD**—scratched, small dents, and dirty.
- **VERY GOOD**—few scratches, no dents, rust or warpage; very clean.
- **EXCELLENT**—minute scratches or nicks; no dents or rust; exceptionally clean.
- **LIKE NEW**—free of blemishes, nicks or scratches; original condition throughout, with vibrant colors; only faint signs of handling or use; price includes original box.
- **NEW**—brand new, absolutely unmarred, all original and unused, in original packaging with all paperwork provided by the manufacturer.
- **CP (C**urrent **P**roduction) means that the item is now being advertised, manufactured, or is currently available from retail stores.
- **NRS (N**o **R**ecorded **S**ales) means that we do not know the current market value of the item. The item may be very scarce and bring a substantial premium over items in its general class, or it may be relatively common but unnoticed. Usually NRS listings occur when an older and previously unknown item is first reported, although we are still discovering relatively common variations that have not been previously reported. If you have confirmable information about the value of an NRS item, please write to us.
- **NM (N**ot **M**anufactured) means that the item may have been cataloged or otherwise advertised, but it was not produced.

● Good	Exc	Cond/$
18	55	_____
33	115	_____
24	70	_____
5	15	_____
9 12	48	_____

TOY TRAIN COLLECTING

Excerpted from the Kalmbach Book *Toy Train Collecting and Operating: An Introduction to the Hobby*, by John Grams

How to Start Collecting Toy Trains

Who collects toy trains? Most of today's toy train collectors have simply retained their love of trains from youth and continued to build upon it, going through various stages, changes, or specializations along the way. Others have experienced a rekindling of their childhood enthusiasm later in life, when they had children or grandchildren to share in the hobby.

As few hobbyists can afford to purchase everything produced by a particular manufacturer, most collectors choose a specific concentration of toy trains to collect. Collectors often narrow their focus to:

One particular gauge or scale
A specific manufacturer's products
A certain era of toy train production
One class of locomotive, rolling stock, accessory, or an individual road name

Where to Buy and Sell Toy Trains

The following suggested sources of old toy trains are tried and true. They are presented as starting points as you enter this fascinating and engrossing hobby.

Private homes, garage sales, estate sales
Classified ads in newspapers and magazines
Mail order
Hobby shops
Swap meets and train shows
Auctions
Antique shops
Trades with other collectors

How to Buy Toy Trains

While geared to the basic circumstances of swap meets, these guidelines will serve the uninitiated train buyer in other places and situations as well. Although they resemble flea markets and gypsy camps on the surface, these train events usually have rules governing them. Most are sponsored by groups or organizations that have a vested interest in promoting the hobby, and they are concerned about scam artists bilking their customer-guests.

Most regular dealers are fairly honest, or at least try to be fair. Many are there primarily because they enjoy the hobby, too. Don't expect trade-ins, unlimited return privileges, layaways, or gift wrap. Few dealers are equipped to handle credit card purchases. And don't be surprised if they refuse to take your check. The first rule of the swap meet game: CASH AND CARRY.

What you see is what you get. All swap meet merchandise is sold as-is. While flaws and malfunctions should be noted, don't assume anything. Look over the merchandise carefully. Note the flaws. Ask questions about it before you start negotiating. Is it all original or does it include reproduced or remanufactured parts? Does it come with an original box? Does it work? Ask to take it to the test track so you can check the performance. Your best assurance is to buy from a dealer who has a good reputation or attends the meets regularly.

That brings us to the negotiation. Some dealers hold firmly to their ticket prices, considering them to be fair appraisals of market value. Others believe that dickering is part of the process of selling. A third group doesn't believe in ticket prices at all and will give you oral quotes if you ask. Give these dealers a wide berth unless you really know what you are doing.

The key to successful bargaining is in making a reasonable offer. Chiseling 10 to 15 percent from the ticket price in good-faith negotiation will probably be acceptable to most dealers. Some will consider larger discounts, but that is hard to predict. Package deals are good. Volume buying will often get you a few more total percentage points.

A dealer's willingness to negotiate on price can be contingent on many variables. Here's a list of the more common ones:

Price of the item
Rarity of the item
Length of time the dealer has carried the item
Volume of traffic at the meet
Length of time into the meet
Season of the year

One final bit of advice: Don't walk around a swap meet thumbing through your pocket price guide. That's a sure sign you're either ripe for picking or looking for an argument. The most vulnerable buyer is a neophyte with a book in his hand.

Preserving Toy Trains

As your collection grows, you will undoubtedly take more interest in maintaining its condition and value. How you choose to deal with this issue may well be one of the most important decisions you make regarding your collection.

Many would have you believe that toy trains should be kept only in a temperature- and humidity-controlled environment, free of dust and pollution, and away from direct sunlight. These trains were produced as toys. Although not indestructible, they are inherently tough.

High humidity can cause rust, but it is easily controlled using a small dehumidifier. Temperature, too, is only a factor in the extreme. And as far as dust, pollution, and direct sunlight are concerned, you need only look for practical solutions such as soft brushes, cans of compressed air, or in worst cases, mild soap and water or furniture polish.

In this report you'll find a number of features we've devised to help you gather an accurate assessment of the current market for S Gauge toy trains.

With the growing popularity of on-line auctions, you'll certainly want to read through the **CTT Market Basket Recap** for review and analysis of both conventional and on-line auction prices. And to wrap up the report, we've included the **S Gauge Marketplace** segment to bring you an overview of market activity.

CTT MARKET BASKET RECAP

by Bob Keller, associate editor for *Classic Toy Trains* magazine.

Conventional Auctions

"Brick and mortar" auctions are held around the country, all year long. You get to see the goods up close and personal, you get to soak up the atmosphere of collectors on the prowl, and you are able to find both A-Number-One quality products as well as bottom feeder gear, all in a single room. Some of the more established firms include Lloyd Ralston Toys of Stratford, Conn., Stout auctions of Indianapolis, Ind., and New England Toy Train Exchange of Bridgeport, Conn. These are highly reputable outfits and you can buy and sell through them with confidence.

In an effort to stay competitive with eBay, many conventional auction houses now allow internet absentee bidding and a few offer "live" internet bidding.

Some interesting values from conventional auctions include:

Engines, rolling stock, accessories & sets
Set no. 5580 with OBs $800; No. 26421 accessory pack $675; No. 48496 orange Monsanto tank car $600; No. 332AC Union Pacific 4-8-4 $500; No. 789 baggage smasher $500; No. 49600 Union Pacific Pony express set $400; No. 346 Nickel Plate 0-8-0 $350; No. 752 Seaboard coal loader $300; Nos. 21918 and -1 Seaboard Baldwin switchers $275; No. 799 Union station $250; No. 342DC Nickel Plate 0-8-0 $250: No. 21573 New Haven EP5 electric $225; No. 973 Milk car with platform $225; No. 21158 blue 0-4-0 $200; Nos. 466 Comet Alco with 960, 962, and 963 blue-stripe passenger cars $195; Nos. 477 and 478 Silver Flash Alcos $165; No. 21164 Prestone Car Care 4-4-2 and tender $150

Internet Auctions

The internet is a 24/7 train show. While you might not be able to score the "steals" you could have a few years back, it is hard to beat, if for no other reason, as a source of information and images of things that are on the market today, not stuck in someone's collection. The leader in the field is eBay, though Charles Siegel's Choochooauctions.com is another great source for instant gratification via modem!

Some interesting internet auction results include:

Engines, rolling stock, and sets

No. 20480 Santa Fe Chief set w/OB $3,550; No. 20370 Northern Pacific set $1,550; No. 21129 New York Central Hudson $1,225; No. 500T Circus set $1,026; No. 21139 Union Pacific 4-8-4 Northern $785; No. 21925 Union Pacific diesels $650; Nos. 8150/8152 Daylight diesel and matching passenger cars $625; No. 49601 Missouri Pacific Eagle set $575; No. 160 station platform w/box $561; No. 8153/8154/8155 Baltimore & Ohio set $560; No. 20425 Pennsylvania switcher set $550; No. 371 American Flyer Lines GP7 diesel $536; $520; No. 21537 New Haven EP-5 electric $504; No. 375 GM GP7 diesel $500; No. 372 Union Pacific GP7 diesel $493; No. 48T Royal Blue set w/boxes $481; No. 296 New Haven 4-6-2 Pacific $470; No. 24425 BAR refrigerator car $455; No. 48926 Western Pacific Zephyr set $455; No. 374/375 Texas & Pacific GP7 diesel set $440; No. 718 mail pickup set $356

Accessories

No. 594 animated track gang $1,005; No. 789 Baggage smasher $479; No. 751 log loader $346; No. 30B transformer $307; No 19085 Gilbert highway system $260; No. 587 block control system (1940-41, 1948-46) $227; No. 23760 highway flasher (mint in the box) $212; No. 23759 danger bell signal $180; No. 23830 Piggy back car unloader w/OB $161; No. 49807 Seaboard coal loader $153; No. 715 automatic unloader w/OB $153; No. 773 oil derrick w/OB $152; No. 23780 Gabe the Lamplighter

The Auction Market

While there are market forces at work effecting the S gauge community, they haven't been as volatile as those striking the O gauge realm. The world of S gauge hasn't seen the vast quantities of over-produced trains that their cohorts collecting three-rail gear have experienced, and the payoff has been a stable sales world for sellers of modern trains and vintage pieces alike.

Generally, sales of postwar and modern era S gauge trains are not at their peak prices from the 1990s, but a tremendous number of trains are still changing hands. As noted in last year's price guide, senior collectors liquidating their inventories injected a large quantity of top-of-the-line sets, trains, and associated products into the marketplace. Items in first rate condition sold quickly for excellent prices, and many collectors and operators were able to upgrade their fleets as other, slightly lower grades were circulated.

So the better goods still command a premium price; but unless it is blemish free or rare, the market is one favoring the buyers.

S Gauge Marketplace: Is modern Flyer dead?

Not the last time I checked, it was just in cryo-freeze. But things are beginning to heat up now!

Lionel's catalogs for 2002 and 2003 have seen Lionel offer the first PA-powered passenger set in some time, the return of the Baldwin switcher (nos. 48034 Seaboard and 48035 Santa Fe), and the no. 49011 "Moe and Joe" operating flatcar. The rest of the rolling stock is pretty conventional—but at least it is Flyer, and it is new Flyer.

There are a ton of repro Flyer accessories out from Lionel (frankly, because there is a market for them in O gauge....) like the 49814 floodlight tower, 49810 log loader, 49813 baggage smasher, and 49812 talking station. I say "Keep 'em coming!"

The Queen Mother of new Flyer products was alluded to in the 2003 Vol. 1 catalog, but not announced till the 2003 Vol. 2 catalog: A Mikado 2-8-2 available as a passenger set in the Baltimore & Ohio road name, or a separate sale in New York Central colors.

What about Flyer's competition?

American Models of South Lyon, Mich., has the largest inventory of available locomotive models in S gauge: Alco PAs, FAs, and RS-3s; Baldwin S-12s and GG1s; and EMD GP9/18s, FP-7s, GP35s, E-8s, F-40s, and SD-60s; the Fairbanks-Morse Train Master, and three styles of steam power, a conventional 4-6-2, a streamlined 4-6-2, and a streamlined 4-6-4 Hudson! Choices, choices, choices!

One of the firm's most popular locomotives, the Pennsylvania GG-1, has been re-released in the silver, black, and Tuscan paint scheme. With matching Budd cars, this version of The Congressional will be one of the most striking passenger sets anywhere.

In 2003 S-Helper Service of Cliffwood, N.J., released an EMD F-7 that is as beautiful a piece as was ever produced—regardless of scale. The chrome version of the Santa Fe is—as the fashion divas might say—"to die for." The firm keeps cranking out some of the most artistically rendered private owner refrigerator cars ever made, and their release of composite hoppers are enough to keep most operators happy. On the horizon is a 2-8-0 Consolidation that will be available in nine road names, and an EMD E-7 AB diesel outfit available undecorated or in 10 road names.

In the nuts and bolts area, S-Helper is offering no. 5 S-Trax switches as well as rail joiners for mating American Flyer track with their sophisticated track and roadbed system. You'll also find SHS offering your choice of two track cleaner cars.

And the new kid on the block, K-Line. Huh? Sure, they've been making Flyer-style S gauge track forever, but now they are dipping into the world of S gauge by offering some re-worked Marx 8-inch freight cars with S gauge trucks and couplers. The cars include boxcars in 12 road names and three-dome tank cars in four names. The price? $19.95 each.

		Good	Exc	Cond/$
American Flyer Circus Coach See (649)				
American Flyer Circus Flatcar See (643)				
Borden's Flatcar Pike Master couplers See (24575)				
Buffalo Hunt Gondola, *63-64*		4	12	____
C&NWRWY 42597 w/ link couplers See (628)				
C&NWRWY 42597 w/ knuckle couplers See (928) or 934				
Freight Ahead Caboose, *63*		3	10	____
G. Fox & Co. See (633F)				
Keystone See (24067)				
New Haven w/ pipes, Pike Master couplers See (24564)				
Pennsylvania See (24130)				
Rocket Launcher and USM See (25056)				
Simmons See (24420)				
Undecorated Flatcar body (See 24575)				
Virginian See (632)				
Washington See (21089)				
1	25-watt Transformer, *49-52*	1	3	____
1	35-watt Transformer, *56*	4	8	____
1A	40-watt Transformer, *57 u*	3	9	____
1½	45-watt Transformer, *53*	1	4	____
1½	50-watt Transformer, *54-55*	1	4	____
1½B	50-watt Transformer, *56*	1	4	____
2	75-watt Transformer, *47-53*	2.50	8	____
2B	75-watt Transformer, *47-48*	2.50	10	____
3	50-watt Transformer, *46 u*	1.50	5	____
4B	100-watt Transformer, *49-56*	10	22	____
5	50-watt Transformer, *46*	1.50	5	____
5A	50-watt Transformer, *46*	1.50	5	____
5B	50-watt Transformer, *46*	2.50	5	____
6	75-watt Transformer, *46*	1	5	____
6A	75-watt Transformer, *46*	1	5	____
7	75-watt Transformer, *46 u*	2	7	____
7B	75-watt Transformer, *46*	2	7	____
8B	100-watt Transformer, *46-52*	12	31	____
9B	150-watt Transformer, *46*	18	34	____
10	DC Inverter, *46*	6	17	____
11	Circuit Breaker, *46*	3	11	____
12B	250-watt Transformer, *46-52*	31	95	____
13	Circuit Breaker, *52-55*	4	7	____
14	Rectiformer, *47, 49*	8	31	____
15	Rectifier, *48-52*	5	24	____
15B	110-watt Transformer, *53*	13	38	____
16	Rectiformer, *50*	10	33	____
16B	190-watt Transformer, *53*	30	70	____
16B	175-watt Transformer, *54-56*	23	60	____
16C	35-watt Transformer, *58*	6	17	____
17B	190-watt Transformer, *52*	31	75	____
18	Filter, *50 u*		NRS	____

		Good	Exc	Cond/S
18B	175-watt Transformer, *54-56*	24	75	___
18B	190-watt Transformer, *53*	29	95	___
19B	300-watt Transformer, *52-55*	48	130	___
20	See (247)20			
21	Imitation Grass, *49-50*	15	24	___
21A	Imitation Grass, *51-56*	15	26	___
22	Scenery Gravel, *49-56*	13	21	___
23	Artificial Coal, *49-56*	14	22	___
24	Rainbow Wire, *49-56*	3	9	___
25	Smoke Cartridge, *47-56*	5	15	___
26	Service Kit, *52-56*	7	25	___
27	Track Cleaning Fluid, *52-56*	2.50	7	___
28	Track Ballast, *50*	5	11	___
28A	Track Ballast, *51-53*	5	12	___
29	Imitation Snow, *50*	45	100	___
29A	Imitation Snow, *51-53*	50	110	___
30	Highway Signs, *49-52*	42	145	___
30	See (247)30			
30B	300-watt Transformer, *53-56*	75	200	___
31	Railroad Signs, *49-50*	80	250	___
31A	Railroad Signs, *51-52*	75	190	___
32	City Street Equipment, *49-50*	55	190	___
32A	Park set, *51*	55	200	___
33	Passenger and Train Figure set, *51-52*	75	215	___
34	Railway Figure set, *53*	105	770	___
35	Brakeman w/ lantern, *50-52*	95	170	___
40	See (247)40			
40	Smoke set, *53-56*	2.50	4	___
50	District School, *53-54*	55	200	___
50	See (247)50			
55	See (240)55			
65	See (245)65			
88	See (210)88			
100	Step Display, *48*	55	250	___
100	Universal Lock-on		NRS	___
160	Station Platform, *53*	145	395	___
161	Bungalow, *53*	115	270	___
162	Factory, *53*	80	255	___
163	Flyerville Station, *53*	110	195	___
164	Red Barn, *53*	105	400	___
165	Grain Elevator, *53*	50	250	___
166	Church, *53*	95	290	___
167	Town hall, *53*	105	335	___
168	Hotel, *53*	120	375	___
234	See (21)234			
247	Tunnel, *46-48*	20	34	___
248	Tunnel, *46-48*	20	34	___
249	Tunnel, *47-56*	14	40	___

		Good	Exc	Cond/$
263	PRR 0-6-0 Switcher, *57*		NM	____
270	News and Frank Stand, *52-53*	50	135	____
271	Three-Piece "Whistle Stop" set, *52-53*	65	185	____
271-1	1) Waiting Station, *52-53*	21	55	____
271-2	2) Refreshment Booth, *52-53*	21	55	____
271-3	3) Newsstand, *52-53*	21	55	____
272	Glendale Station and Newsstand, *52-53*	65	215	____
273	Suburban Railroad Station, *52-53*	65	205	____
274	Harbor Junction Freight Station, *52-53*	55	205	____
275	Eureka Diner, *52-53*	45	200	____
282	CNW 4-6-2 Pacific, *52-53*			
	(A) "American Flyer", *52*	38	85	____
	(B) w/ coal pusher, *53*	44	95	____
283	CNW 4-6-2 Pacific, *54-57*	29	90	____
285	CNW 4-6-2 Pacific, *52*	42	130	____
287	CNW 4-6-2 Pacific, *54*	21	75	____
289	CNW 4-6-2 Pacific, *56 u*	80	280	____
290	American Flyer 4-6-2 Pacific, *49-51*	28	90	____
293	NYNH&H 4-6-2 Pacific, *53-58*			
	(A) Reverse in tender, *53-57*	45	125	____
	(B) Reverse in cab, *57 u*	90	195	____
295	American Flyer 4-6-2 Pacific, *51*	70	210	____
296	NYNH&H 4-6-2 Pacific, *55 u*	75	310	____
299	Reading 4-4-2 Atlantic, *54 u*	42	170	____
300	Reading 4-4-2 Atlantic, *46-47, 52*			
	(A) "Reading", *46-47*	19	70	____
	(B) Other variations, *47, 52*	15	49	____
300AC	Reading 4-4-2 Atlantic, *49-50*	15	46	____
301	Reading 4-4-2 Atlantic, *53*	15	46	____
302	RL 4-4-2 Atlantic (mv), *48, 51-53*			
	(A) Smoke in tender		NRS	____
	(B) Smoke in boiler	14	50	____
	(C) Plastic	15	50	____
302AC	Reading Lines 4-4-2 Atlantic (mv), *48, 50-52*	15	50	____
303	Reading 4-4-2 Atlantic, *54-56*	15	60	____
305	Reading 4-4-2, *51*		NM	____
307	Reading 4-4-2 Atlantic, *54-57*	16	50	____
308	Reading 4-4-2 Atlantic, *56*	24	90	____
310	PRR 4-6-2 Pacific, *46-48*	39	115	____
312	PRR 4-6-2 Pacific (mv), *46-48, 51-52*			
	(A) "Pennsylvania", s-i-t, *46*	55	155	____
	(B) Other variations	65	135	____
312AC	PRR 4-6-2 Pacific, *49-51*	50	125	____
313	PRR 4-6-2 Pacific, *55-57*	55	210	____
314AW	PRR 4-6-2 Pacific, *49-50*	85	305	____
315	PRR 4-6-2 Pacific, *52*	75	255	____
316	PRR 4-6-2 Pacific, *53-54*	65	215	____
320	NYC 4-6-4 Hudson, *46-47*	50	165	____

		Good	Exc	Cond/$
321	NYC 4-6-4 Hudson, *46-47*	47	205	____
322	NYC 4-6-4 Hudson, *46-49*			
	(A) "New York Central", *46*	41	185	____
	(B) "American Flyer Lines", *47-49*	35	145	____
322AC	NYC 4-6-4 Hudson, *49-57*	41	145	____
324AC	NYC 4-6-4 Hudson, *50*	65	225	____
325AC	NYC 4-6-4 Hudson, *51*	55	170	____
K325	NYC 4-6-4 Hudson, *52*			
	(A) Early coupler riveted to truck	155	325	____
	(B) Other variations	50	180	____
326	NYC 4-6-4 Hudson, *53-57*			
	(A) Small motor	55	200	____
	(B) Large motor	85	265	____
332	Union Pacific 4-8-4, Northern, *46-49*			
	(A) AC, "Union Pacific" s-i-t, *46*		NRS	____
	(B) AC "American Flyer Lines", *47-48*	150	400	____
	(C) DC "American Flyer Lines", *48-49*	150	465	____
	(D) DC silver lettering, *47*	1050	2400	____
332AC	Union Pacific 4-8-4 Northern, *51*	150	420	____
332DC	Union Pacific 4-8-4 Northern, *49*	135	495	____
334DC	Union Pacific 4-8-4 Northern, *50*	150	455	____
K335	Union Pacific 4-8-4 Northern, *52*	130	415	____
336	Union Pacific 4-8-4 Northern, *53-56*			
	(A) Small motor	130	465	____
	(B) Large motor	145	500	____
342	NKP 0-8-0 Switcher, *46-48, 52*			
	(A) "Nickel Plate Road" s-i-t, *46*		NRS	____
	(B) "American Flyer Lines" s-i-t, *47*	115	435	____
	(C) Same as (B), but DC	110	455	____
	(D) "American Flyer Lines" s-i-b, *48*	95	355	____
	(E) "American Flyer", *52*	95	380	____
342AC	NKP 0-8-0 Switcher, *49-51*	100	335	____
342DC	NKP 0-8-0 Switcher, *48-50*	100	325	____
343	NKP 0-8-0 Switcher, *53-58*			
	(A) Reverse in tender, *53-54*	110	340	____
	(B) Reverse on motor, *54, 56*	125	400	____
346	NKP 0-8-0 Switcher, *55*	205	590	____
350	Royal Blue 4-6-2 Pacific (mv), *48, 50*			
	(A) Wire handrails, *48*	50	175	____
	(B) Cast handrails, *50*	43	155	____
353	AF Circus 4-6-2 Pacific, *50-51*	125	475	____
354	Silver Bullet 4-6-2 Pacific, *54*	60	190	____
355	CNW Baldwin, *56-57*			
	(A) Unpainted green plastic	65	140	____
	(B) Green-painted plastic	115	305	____
356	Silver Bullet 4-6-2 Pacific, *53*			
	(A) Chrome	65	215	____
	(B) Satin-silver paint	60	65	____

		Good	Exc	Cond/$
360/361	Santa Fe PA/PB, *50-51*			
	(A) Chromed, *50*	70	265	___
	(B) Chromed w/ handrails, *50*	120	570	___
	(C) Silver-painted, *51*	70	230	___
360/364	Santa Fe PA/PB, *50-51*			
	(A) Silver-painted, "Santa Fe", *50*	70	225	___
	(B) Other variations		NRS	___
360/361/360	SP PA/PB/PA Cutout Pilots, u		NRS	___
370	GM AF GP-7, *50-53*			
	(A) w/ link coupler bars	60	165	___
	(B) w/ knuckle couplers	65	190	___
371	GM AF GP-7, *54*	105	220	___
372	Union Pacific GP-7, *55-57*			
	(A) "Built by Gilbert"	115	260	___
	(B) "Made by American Flyer"	135	350	___
374/375	Texas & Pacific GP-7, *54-55*			
	(A) Sheet metal frame	175	460	___
	(B) Die-cast frame	160	430	___
375	GM AF GP-7, *53*	490	1300	___
377/378	Texas & Pacific GP-7, *56-57*	175	510	___
(405)	Silver Streak PA, *52*	85	295	___
440	Lamp	1.50	5	___
441	Lamp	1.50	5	___
442	Lamp	1.50	5	___
443	Lamp	1.50	8	___
444	Lamp	1.50	5	___
450	Track Terminal, *46-48*	1.50	5	___
451	Lamp	1.50	5	___
452	Lamp	1.50	5	___
453	Lamp, *46-48*			
	(A) One bulb	1.50	5	___
	(B) Three bulbs	1.50	5	___
460	Bulbs, *51, 53-54*	34	120	___
461	Lamp	2	7	___
466	Comet, PA, *53-55*			
	(A) Chromed, *53*	85	225	___
	(B) Silver-painted, decal, *54-55*	75	220	___
	(C) Silver-painted, w/ heat-stamped lett.	90	280	___
467	Comet PB, *55**		8000	___
470/471/473	SF PA/PB/PA, *53-58*			
	(A) Chromed, *53*	130	455	___
	(B) Silver-painted, *54-57*	115	425	___
	(C) Silver-painted, integral steps	245	570	___
472	Santa Fe PA, *56*	110	305	___
474/475	Rocket PA/PA, *53-55*			
	(A) Chromed, *53*	125	340	___
	(B) Silver-painted, *54-55*	110	350	___
476	Rocket PB, *55**		NRS	___

		Good	Exc	Cond/$
477/478	Silver Flash PA/PB, *53-54*			
	(A) Chromed, *53*	170	570	____
	(B) Silver-painted, *54*	165	500	____
479	Silver Flash PA, *55*	80	290	____
480	Silver Flash PB, *55**		1100	____
481	Silver Flash PA, *56*	115	325	____
484/485/486	Santa Fe PA/PB/PA, *56-57*	215	680	____
490/491/493	Northern Pacific PA/PB/PA, *56**	340	1150	____
490/492	Northern Pacific PA/PA, *57*	200	690	____
494/495	New Haven PA/PA, *56*	195	760	____
497	New Haven PA, *57*	105	340	____
499	New Haven GE Electric, *56-57*	105	420	____
500	AFL Combination Car, *52 u*			
	(A) Silver finish	140	570	____
	(B) Chrome finish	100	340	____
501	AFL Passenger Car, *52 u*			
	(A) Silver finish	150	570	____
	(B) Chrome finish	110	370	____
502	AFL Vista Dome Car, *52 u*			
	(A) Silver finish	145	560	____
	(B) Chrome finish	110	370	____
503	AFL Observation Car, *52 u*	155	600	____
520	Knuckle Coupler kit, *54-56*	1.50	5	____
521	Knuckle Coupler kit		45	____
525	Knuckle Coupler Trucks		45	____
526	Knuckle Coupler Trucks		45	____
529	Knuckle Coupler Trucks		45	____
530	Knuckle Coupler Trucks		45	____
532	Knuckle Coupler Trucks		45	____
541	Fuses, *46*		NRS	____
561	Billboard Horn, *55-56*	25	65	____
566	Whistling Billboard, *51-55*	16	55	____
568	Whistling Billboard, *56*	18	40	____
571	Truss Bridge, *55-56*	11	44	____
573	American Flyer Talking Station Record		NRS	____
577	Whistling Billboard, *46-50*			
	(A) Circus, *46-47*	21	75	____
	(B) Fox Mart, *47*		1550	____
	(C) Trains, *50*	24	44	____
578	Station Figure set, *46-52*	55	170	____
579	Single Street Lamp, *46-49*	10	50	____
580	Double Street Lamp, *46-49*	12	55	____
581	Girder Bridge, *46-56*	11	35	____
582	Blinker Signal, *46-48*	55	150	____
583	Electromatic Crane, *46-49*	65	205	____
583A	Electromatic Crane, *50-53*	65	205	____
584	Bell Danger Signal, *46-47*	190	730	____
585	Tool Shed, *46-52*	23	70	____

		Good	Exc	Cond/$
586F	Wayside Station, *46-56*	29	115	____
587	Block Signal, *46-47*	70	240	____
588	Semaphore Block Signal, *46-48*	650	1900	____
589	Passenger and Freight Station, *46-56*			
	(A) Green-painted roof	16	65	____
	(B) Black-painted roof	15	85	____
590	Control Tower, *55-56*	23	75	____
591	Crossing Gate, *46-48*	21	85	____
592	Crossing Gate, *49-50*	24	90	____
592A	Crossing Gate, *51-53*	27	90	____
593	Signal Tower, *46-54*	36	85	____
594	Animated Track Gang, *46-47**	570	2250	____
596	Operating Water Tank, *46-56*	39	80	____
598	Talking Station Record, *46-56*	10	21	____
599	Talking Station Record, *56*	11	35	____
600	Crossing Gate w/ bell, *54-56*	30	95	____
605	American Flyer Lines Flatcar, *53*	10	45	____
606	American Flyer Lines Crane, *53*	15	55	____
607	AFL Work and Boom Car, *53*	9	44	____
609	American Flyer Lines Flatcar, *53*	10	44	____
612	Freight Passenger Station w/ Crane, *46-51, 53-54*	50	120	____
613	Great Northern Boxcar, *53*	21	80	____
620	Southern Gondola, *53*	22	90	____
621	½ Straight Track, *46-48*	0.20	0.50	____
622	½ Curved Track, *46-48*	0.15	0.45	____
622	GAEX Boxcar, *53**	16	75	____
623	Illinois Central Reefer, *53**	11	33	____
625	Shell Tank Car, *46-50*			
	(A) Orange tanks	370	800	____
	(B) Black tanks	10	40	____
	(C) Silver tanks	6	28	____
625	Gulf Tank Car, *51-53*	8	24	____
625G	Gulf Tank Car, *51-53 u*	9	27	____
627	C&NWRY Flatcar (mv), *46-50*	10	28	____
627	American Flyer Lines Flatcar, *50*	14	46	____
(628)	C&NWRY Flatcar, *46-53*			
	(A) Metal	8	31	____
	(B) Wood	13	50	____
629	Missouri Pacific Stock Car (mv), *46-53*	9	35	____
630	Reading Caboose (mv), *46-52*	5	16	____
630	American Flyer Caboose, *52*	9	38	____
630	American Flyer Lines Caboose, *53*	8	26	____
631	Texas & Pacific Gondola, *46-53*			
	(A) Green unpainted	8	17	____
	(B) Dark gray unpainted, *48 u*	70	280	____
	(C) Red-painted, *52 u*	27	135	____
	(D) Green-painted, *46-52*	4	19	____

		Good	Exc	Cond/S
(632)	Virginian Hopper, *46*	32	115	____
632	Lehigh New England Hopper, *46-53*			
	(A) Gray-painted, die-cast, *46*	30	125	____
	(B) Black plastic, *46*	8	26	____
	(C) Gray plastic	4	16	____
	(D) White plastic	33	125	____
	(E) Painted body	9	27	____
633	Baltimore & Ohio Boxcars (mv), *46-52*	10	25	____
633	Baltimore & Ohio Reefers (mv), *46-52*			
	(A) Red, *52 u*	39	150	____
	(B) Tuscan, *52 u*	45	155	____
633F	G. Fox & Co. Boxcar, *47 u* *	990	2850	____
634	C&NWRY Floodlight (mv), *46-49, 53*	11	40	____
635	C&NWRY Crane, *46-48*	15	65	____
(635)	C&NWRY Crane, *48-49*			
	(A) Yellow cab	11	50	____
	(B) Red cab	95	325	____
	(C) Black roof		NRS	____
636	Erie Flatcar, *48-53*			
	(A) Die-cast metal frame	13	40	____
	(B) Pressed-wood frame, *53 u*	65	285	____
637	MKT Boxcar (mv), *49-53* *	8	36	____
638	American Flyer Caboose (mv), *49-52*	4	10	____
638	American Flyer Lines Caboose, *53*	5	15	____
639	American Flyer Boxcars (mv), *49-52*			
	(A) Yellow body	7	20	____
	(B) Tuscan body	16	75	____
639	American Flyer Reefers (mv), *51-52*			
	(A) Yellow body	6	18	____
	(B) Unpainted cream plastic body	47	190	____
640	American Flyer Hopper, *49-53*			
	(A) White lettering	4	14	____
	(B) Black lettering	4	18	____
	(C) White plastic body w/ black lettering	14	60	____
640	Wabash Hopper, *53*	9	34	____
641	American Flyer Gondola, *49-52*			
	(A) Red-painted or unpainted plastic	10	24	____
	(B) Gray unpainted, *51 u*	50	265	____
641	Frisco Gondola, *53*	11	31	____
642	American Flyer Boxcars, *51-52*	10	21	____
642	American Flyer Reefers, *52 u*	7	24	____
642	Seaboard Boxcar, *53*	11	35	____
(643)	American Flyer Circus Flatcar, *50-53* *			
	(A) Yellow, metal	75	265	____
	(B) Yellow, wood	90	375	____
	(C) Red, metal	120	455	____
644	American Flyer Crane, *50-53*			
	(A) Red cab, black boom, *50*	35	130	____

		Good	Exc	Cond/$
	(B) Red cab, green boom, *50*	22	85	____
	(C) Tuscan-painted cab, green boom, *50-51*	27	90	____
	(D) Black cab, boom	20	75	____
645	AF Work and Boom Car, *50*	16	45	____
645A	AFL Work and Boom Car, *51-53*	16	46	____
(646)	Erie Floodlight, *50-53*			
	(A) Green-painted die-cast generator, *50*	47	240	____
	(B) Other variations	18	55	____
647	Northern Pacific Reefer, *52-53*	13	48	____
648	American Flyer Flatcar, *52-54*	10	35	____
(649)	AF Circus Passenger Car (mv), *50-52*	44	120	____
650	New Haven Pullman Car (mv), *46-53*			
	(A) Red or green w/ plastic frame	21	85	____
	(B) Red or green w/ die-cast frame	22	65	____
	(C) Red or green w/ sheet metal frame	15	47	____
651	New Haven Baggage Car (mv), *46-53*			
	(A) Red or green w/ plastic frame	12	60	____
	(B) Red or green w/ die-cast frame	12	55	____
	(C) Red or green w/ sheet metal frame	11	50	____
652	Pullman (mv), *46-53*			
	(A) Red, tuscan, or green, short trucks	41	150	____
	(B) Red or green, long trucks	65	235	____
	(C) Red, tuscan, or green, "Pikes Peak"	48	170	____
653	Pullman (mv), *46-53*			
	(A) Red or green, long trucks	65	220	____
	(B) Red, tuscan, or green, short trucks	40	145	____
654	Pullman Observation Car (mv), *46-53*			
	(A) Red or green, long trucks	60	215	____
	(B) Red, tuscan, or green, short trucks	41	140	____
655	Silver Bullet Passenger Car, *53*			
	(A) Chrome	25	115	____
	(B) Satin aluminum	20	95	____
655	AFL Passenger Car, *53*			
	(A) Tuscan	22	70	____
	(B) Green	22	70	____
660	AFL Combination Car, *50-52*			
	(A) Extruded aluminum shell	18	60	____
	(B) Chrome-finished, plastic shell	27	95	____
	(C) Satin silver		NRS	____
661	AFL Passenger Car, *50-52*			
	(A) Extruded aluminum shell	37	90	____
	(B) Chrome-finished, plastic shell	44	105	____
	(C) Satin silver		NRS	____
662	AFL Vista Dome Car, *50-52*			
	(A) Extruded aluminum shell	22	70	____
	(B) Chrome-finished, plastic shell	30	95	____
663	AFL Observation Car, *50-52*	22	70	____
668	Manual Switch, LH, *53-55*	5	9	____

		Good	Exc	Cond/$
669	Manual Switch, RH, *53-55*	5	9	___
670	Track Trip, *55-56*	2	15	___
678	RC Switch, LH, *53-56*	7	17	___
679	RC Switch, RH, *53-56*	6	16	___
680	Curved Track, *46-48*	0.20	0.45	___
681	Straight Track, *46-48*	0.25	0.50	___
688	RC Switches, pair, *46-48*	20	50	___
690	Track Terminal, *46-56*	0.50	1	___
691	Steel Pins, *46-48*	0.45	0.90	___
692	Fiber Pins, *46-48*	0.25	0.75	___
693	Track Locks, *48-56*	0.05	0.15	___
694	Coupler, Truck, Wheels, Axles, *46-53*	2.50	9	___
695	Track Trip, *46*	6	13	___
695	Reverse Loop Relay, *55-56*	26	80	___
696	Track Trip, *55-57*			
	(A) Plastic shoe	10	22	___
	(B) Die-cast shoe	10	28	___
697	Track Trip, *50-54*	4	11	___
698	Reverse Loop Kit, *49-50, 52-54*	17	65	___
700	Straight Track, *46-56*	0.50	1	___
701	½ Straight Track, *46-56*	0.25	0.80	___
702	Curved Track, *46-56*	0.15	0.35	___
703	½ Curved Track, *46-56*	0.10	0.20	___
704	Manual Uncoupler, *52-56*	0.30	0.55	___
705	RC Uncoupler, *46-47*	1	4	___
706	RC Uncoupler, *48-56*	0.55	3	___
707	Track Terminal, *46-59*	0.15	0.80	___
708	Air Chime Whistle Control, *51-56*	3	10	___
709	Lockout Eliminator, *50-55*	2	7	___
710	Steam Whistle Control, *55-56*	8	39	___
710	Automatic Track Section, *46-47*	0.55	1.50	___
711	Mail Pickup, *46-47*	9	19	___
712	Special Rail Section, *47-56*	0.50	1	___
713	Special Rail Section w/ mail bag hook, *47-56*	8	26	___
714	Log Unloading Car Flatcar, *51-54*	16	70	___
715	American Flyer Lines Flatcar (mv), *46-54*			
	(A) Armored car	24	120	___
	(B) Manoil Coupe	20	75	___
	(C) Racer	20	75	___
716	American Flyer Lines Hopper, *46-51*			
	(A) 46	6	34	___
	(B) 47-51	6	26	___
717	American Flyer Lines Flatcar, *46-52*	13	55	___
718	New Haven Mail Pickup (mv), *46-54*			
	(A) Red or green	31	100	___
	(B) Red pickup arm	155	395	___
	(C) Tuscan		NRS	___

No.	Description	Good	Exc	Cond/$
719	CB&Q Hopper Dump Car, *50-54*			
	(A) Tuscan-painted	25	90	____
	(B) Red plastic	30	115	____
720	RC Switches, *46-49*	19	50	____
720A	RC Switches, *50-56*	26	55	____
722	Manual Switches, *46-51*	9	19	____
722A	Manual Switches, *52-56*	9	18	____
725	Crossing, *46-56*	2.50	6	____
726	Straight Rubber Roadbed, *50-56*	0.55	2.50	____
727	Curved Rubber Roadbed, *50-56*	0.45	2	____
728	Re-railer, *56*	2.50	17	____
730	Bumper, *46-56*			
	(A) Green plastic	11	21	____
	(B) Red, *51*	35	135	____
	(C) Green-painted	23	85	____
731	Pike Planning Kit, *52-56*	10	34	____
732	AF Operating Baggage Car, *51-54*			
	(A) Unpainted red or green plastic body	29	85	____
	(B) Green-painted plastic body	34	100	____
734	American Flyer Operating Boxcar, *50-54*	23	80	____
735	NH Animated Station Coach, *52-54*	30	95	____
736	Missouri Pacific Stock Car, *50-54*	10	36	____
(740)	American Flyer Lines Motorized Handcar, *52-54*			
	(A) No decals, no vent holes, *52*	33	110	____
	(B) w/ shield decal	17	75	____
741	AFL Handcar and Shed, motorized unit, *53-54*	75	215	____
(742)	AFL Motorized Handcar, *55-56*	41	145	____
743	See (23)743			
747	Cardboard Trestle Set, u	7	23	____
748	Overhead Foot Bridge, *51-52*			
	(A) Gray/aluminum	10	33	____
	(B) Bluish-silver	28	50	____
748	Girder, Trestle, Tower Bridge, *58 u*	19	44	____
749	Streetlamp set, *50-52*	7	25	____
750	Trestle Bridge, *46-56*	16	70	____
751	Log Loader, *46-50*	42	195	____
751A	Log Loader, *52-53*	47	220	____
752	Seaboard Coaler, *46-50*	110	345	____
752A	Seaboard Coaler, *51-52*	135	345	____
753	Single Trestle Bridge, *52*	16	65	____
753	Mountain, Tunnel, Pass Set, *60 u*	17	39	____
754	Double Trestle Bridge, *50-52*	38	95	____
755	Talking Station, *48-50*			
	(A) Green roof	50	120	____
	(B) Blue roof	85	155	____
758	Sam the Semaphore Man, *49*	29	105	____
758A	Sam the Semaphore Man, *50-56*	34	95	____

		Good	Exc	Cond/$
759	Bell Danger Signal (mv), *53-56*	22	75	___
760	Highway Flasher, *49-56*	9	36	___
761	Semaphore, *49-56*	22	75	___
762	Two in One Whistle, *49-50*	35	95	___
763	Mountain set, *49-50*	46	185	___
764	Express Office, *50-51*	47	155	___
766	Animated Station, *52-54*	55	190	___
K766	Animated Station, *53-55*	55	205	___
767	Roadside Diner, *50-54*	40	110	___
768	Oil Supply Depot, *50-53*			
	(A) "Shell"	40	125	___
	(B) "Gulf"	55	170	___
769	Aircraft Beacon, *50*	16	55	___
769A	Aircraft Beacon, *51-56*	18	65	___
770	Loading Platform, *50-52*	31	90	___
770	Girder Trestle Set, *60 u*	4	18	___
771	Operating Stockyard, *50-54*	46	135	___
K771	Stockyard and Car, *53-56*	50	155	___
772	Water Tower, *50-56*			
	(A) Small tank	30	90	___
	(B) Checkerboard, metal shack	37	130	___
	(C) Checkerboard, plastic shack	55	165	___
773	Oil Derrick, *50-52*			
	(A) "American Flyer", *50*	48	155	___
	(B) "Gulf" logo		NRS	___
774	Floodlight Tower (mv), *51-56*	16	75	___
775	Baggage Platform w/ LC Car, *53-55*	24	95	___
K775	Baggage Platform w/ KC Car, *53-55*	35	125	___
778	Street Lamp set, *53-56*	11	30	___
779	Oil Drum Loader, *55-56*	55	165	___
780	Trestle set, *53-56*	5	18	___
781	Abutment set, *53*	22	65	___
782	Abutment set, *53*	17	05	___
783	Hi-Trestle Sections, *53-56*	5	23	___
784	Hump set, *55*	75	280	___
785	Coal Loader, *55-56*	120	325	___
787	Log Loader, *55-56*	80	305	___
788	Suburban Station, *56*	11	65	___
789	Station and Baggage Smasher, *56-57*	60	275	___
790	Trainorama, *53 u*	48	225	___
792	Terminal, *54-56*	65	195	___
793	Union Station, *55-56*	16	120	___
794	Union Station, *54*	32	125	___
795	Union Station and Terminal, *54*	110	520	___
799	Talking Station, *54-56*	35	190	___
801	Baltimore & Ohio Hopper, *56-57*	11	21	___
802	Illinois Central Reefer, *56-57**	12	26	___

		Good	Exc	Cond/$
803	Santa Fe Boxcar, *56-57*	17	33	____
804	Norfolk & Western Gondola, *56-57*	7	15	____
805	Pennsylvania Gondola, *56-57*	7	15	____
806	American Flyer Lines Caboose, *56-57*	9	12	____
807	Rio Grande Boxcar, *57*			
	(A) Non-opening door	19	38	____
	(B) Opening door		NRS	____
812	See (21)812			
900	NP Combination Car, *56-57**	100	295	____
901	NP Passenger Car, *56-57**	100	295	____
902	NP Vista Dome Car, *56-57**	100	295	____
903	NP Observation Car, *56-57**	100	295	____
904	American Flyer Lines Caboose, *56*	11	25	____
905	American Flyer Lines Flatcar, *54*	11	48	____
906	American Flyer Lines Crane, *54*	16	55	____
907	AFL Work and Boom Car, *54*	12	55	____
909	American Flyer Lines Flatcar, *54*	11	49	____
910	Gilbert Chemical Tank Car, *54**	70	265	____
911	C&O Gondola, *55-57*			
	(A) Silver pipes	10	43	____
	(B) Brown plastic pipes	34	145	____
912	Koppers Tank Car, *55-57*	17	90	____
913	Great Northern Boxcar, *53-58*			
	(A) Decal	14	39	____
	(B) Stamped	14	42	____
914	American Flyer Lines Flatcar, *53-57*	17	70	____
915	American Flyer Lines Flatcar (mv), *53-57*	13	65	____
916	Delaware & Hudson Gondola, *55-56*	8	33	____
918	American Flyer Lines Mail Car, *53-58*			
	(A) "American Flyer Lines"	29	90	____
	(B) "New Haven"	35	120	____
919	CB&Q Hopper Dump Car, *53-56*	23	115	____
920	Southern Gondola, *53-56*	9	32	____
921	CB&Q Hopper, *53-56*	8	34	____
922	GAEX Boxcar, *53-57**			
	(A) Decal	15	43	____
	(B) Stamped	15	50	____
923	Illinois Central Reefer, *54-55**	13	25	____
924	CRP Hopper, *53-56*	8	33	____
925	Gulf Tank Car, *52-57*	13	23	____
926	Gulf Tank Car, *55-57*	11	60	____
(928)	C&NWRY Flatcar, *52-54*			
	(A) Pressed-wood base	24	85	____
	(B) Die-cast base	9	26	____
928	New Haven Flatcar (Log Car), *56 u*	9	37	____
928	New Haven Flatcar (Lumber Car), *56-57*	11	34	____
929	Missouri Pacific Stock Car, *53-56*	10	38	____

		Good	Exc	Cond/$
930	American Flyer Caboose, *52*			
	(A) Early knuckle coupler	28	80	____
	(B) Red	15	55	____
	(C) Tuscan	9	35	____
930	American Flyer Lines Caboose, *53-57*			
	(A) Type I or II body	11	34	____
	(B) Type III body	42	150	____
931	Texas & Pacific Gondola, *52-55*	5	18	____
933	B&O Boxcar, *53-54*	19	55	____
934	American Flyer Lines Caboose, u, *54*	16	60	____
934	C&NWRY Floodlight, *53-54*	10	34	____
934	Southern Pacific Floodlight, *54 u*	14	60	____
935	AFL Bay Window Caboose, *57*	21	100	____
936	Erie Flatcar, *53-54*	12	40	____
936	Pennsylvania Flatcar, *55-57*	40	150	____
937	MKT Boxcar, *53-58**			
	(A) All yellow	9	42	____
	(B) Yellow and brown	9	39	____
938	American Flyer Lines Caboose, *54-55*	5	13	____
940	Wabash Hopper, *53-56*	7	31	____
941	Frisco Lines Gondola, *53-56*	7	22	____
942	Seaboard Boxcar, *54*	10	33	____
944	American Flyer Crane, *52-57*	22	80	____
945	AFL Work and Boom Car, *52-57*	12	50	____
(946)	Erie Floodlight (mv), *53-56*	11	45	____
947	Northern Pacific Reefer, *53-58*	11	43	____
948	AFL Flatcar, *53-56*	11	37	____
951	AFL Baggage Car (mv), *53-57*			
	(A) Red or tuscan	14	48	____
	(B) Green	18	55	____
952	AFL Pullman Car, *53-58*			
	(A) w/o silhouettes, tuscan or green	36	165	____
	(B) w/ silhouettes, tuscan	50	240	____
953	AFL Combination Car, *53-58*			
	(A) w/o silhouettes, tuscan or green	35	160	____
	(B) w/ silhouettes, tuscan	55	235	____
954	AFL Observation Car, *53-56*			
	(A) w/o silhouettes, tuscan or green	36	170	____
	(B) w/ silhouettes, tuscan	105	240	____
955	AFL Passenger Car, *54-55*			
	(A) Satin silver-painted	30	100	____
	(B) Green-painted	31	105	____
	(C) Tuscan-painted w/ silhouettes and "955"	21	100	____
	(D) Tuscan-painted w/ silhouettes and white-outlined windows	29	115	____
956	Monon Flatcar, *56*	21	95	____
957	Erie Operating Boxcar, *57 u*	47	160	____
958	Mobilgas Tank Car, *57 u*	23	105	____

		Good	Exc	Cond/$
960	AFL Columbus Combination Car, *53-56*			
	(A) No color band	30	115	____
	(B) Blue, green, or red band	40	110	____
	(C) Chestnut band	75	260	____
	(D) Orange band	50	185	____
961	AFL Jefferson Pullman Car, *53-58*			
	(A) No color band	40	130	____
	(B) Blue band		NM	____
	(C) Green or red band	39	130	____
	(D) Chestnut band	95	310	____
	(E) Orange band	65	200	____
962	AFL Hamilton Vista Dome Car, *53-58*			
	(A) No color band	40	140	____
	(B) Blue, green, or red band	41	135	____
	(C) Chestnut band	90	310	____
	(D) Orange band	65	195	____
963	AFL Washington Passenger Car, *53-58*			
	(A) No color band	40	140	____
	(B) Blue, green, or red band	36	115	____
	(C) Chestnut band	85	290	____
	(D) Orange band	65	190	____
969	Rocket Launcher Flatcar, *57 u*	21	80	____
970	Seaboard Operating Boxcar, *56-57*	29	75	____
971	Southern Pacific Flatcar, *56-57*	39	155	____
973	Gilbert's Operating Milk Car, *56-57*	55	175	____
974	AFL Operating Boxcar, *53-54*	27	80	____
974	Erie Operating Boxcar, *55*	48	170	____
975	AFL Operating Coach, *54-55*	29	95	____
976	MoPac Operating Cattle Car, *53-62*	25	70	____
977	American Flyer Lines Caboose, *55-57*	28	80	____
978	AFL Grand Canyon Obsv. Car, *56-58*	130	430	____
979	AFL bay window Caboose, *57*	41	140	____
980	Baltimore & Ohio Boxcar, *56-57*	33	125	____
981	Central of Georgia Boxcar, *56-57*			
	(A) Shiny black paint	44	135	____
	(B) Dull black paint	55	170	____
982	BAR Boxcar, *56-57*	48	135	____
983	MoPac Boxcar, *56-57*	48	145	____
984	New Haven Boxcar, *56-57*	30	105	____
985	BM Boxcar, *57*	50	140	____
988	ART Co. Reefer, *56-57*	36	110	____
989	Northwestern Reefer, *56-58*	47	190	____
994	Union Pacific Stock Car, *57*	55	210	____
C1001	WSX Boxcar, *62 u **	260	860	____
1-1024 A	Trestle set, *52 u*	10	44	____
C2001	Post Boxcar, *62 u*	13	46	____
L2001	Game Train 4-4-0, *63*	15	38	____
L2002	Burlington Route 4-4-0, *63 u*	50	230	____

		Good	Exc	Cond/$
L-2004	Rio Grande EMD F-9, *62*	80	220	____
C-2009	Texas & Pacific Gondola, *62-64*			
	(A) Dark green		NRS	____
	(B) Light green	6	21	____
7210	See (636), (646), 936, (946), or (24529)			
21004	PRR 0-6-0 Switcher, *57 u*	95	365	____
21005	PRR 0-6-0 Switcher, *57-58*	125	495	____
(21030)	See 307			
(21034)	See 303			
(21044)	See 313			
(21058)	See 326			
21084	CNW 4-6-2, Pacific, *57 u*	41	150	____
21085	CNW or CMStP&P 4-6-2 Pacific, *58-65*	35	110	____
(210)88	FY&P 4-4-0 Franklin, *59-60*	44	140	____
(21089)	FY&PRR 4-4-0 Wash., *60-61*	65	280	____
21095	NYNH&H 4-6-2 Pacific, *57*		4000	____
21099	NYNH&H 4-6-2 Pacific, *58*	105	375	____
21100	Reading 4-4-2 Atlantic, *57 u*	14	39	____
21105	Reading 4-4-2 Atlantic, *57-58*	17	50	____
21106	Reading 4-4-2 Atlantic, *59 u*	60	200	____
21107	PRR or BN 4-4-2 Atlantic, *64-65 u*	10	38	____
21115	PRR 4-6-2 Pacific, *58*	215	950	____
21129	NYC 4-6-4 Hudson, *58*	235	1150	____
21130	NYC 4-6-4 Hudson, *59-60*	140	365	____
21139	UP 4-8-4 Northern, *58-59*	240	940	____
21140	UP 4-8-4 Northern, *60*	405	1650	____
21145	NKP 0-8-0 Switcher, *58*	165	660	____
21155	Steam 0-6-0 Switcher, *58*	90	390	____
21156	Steam 0-6-0 Switcher, *59*	80	315	____
21158	Steam 0-6-0 Switcher, *60 u*	36	120	____
21160	Reading 4-4-2 Atlantic, *58-60 u*	15	37	____
21161	Reading 4-4-2 Atlantic, *60 u*			
	(A) "American Flyer Lines"	11	27	____
	(B) "Prestone Car Care Express"	65	240	____
21165	Erie 4-4-0, *61-62, 65-66 u*	10	32	____
21166	Burlington Route 4-4-0, *63-64, 65-66 u*			
	(A) White letters	10	25	____
	(B) Black letters	70	215	____
21168	Southern 4-4-0, *61-63*	26	75	____
21205/21205-1	BM twin EMD F-9s, *61, 62 u*			
	(A) Twin A units (u)	110	285	____
	(B) Single unit	75	200	____
21206/21206-1	SF twin EMD F-9s, *62 u*	105	285	____
21207/21207-1	GN twin EMD F-9s, *63-64*	100	320	____
21210	Burlington EMD F-9, *61*	65	250	____
21215/21215-1	UP EMD F-9, *61-62*	95	260	____
21215/21216	UP twin EMD F-9s, *61*		NRS	____

		Good	Exc	Cond/$
(21)234	Chesapeake & Ohio GP-7, *59-61*			
	(A) Long steps	140	490	____
	(B) Short steps	165	590	____
21551	Northern Pacific PA, *58*			
	(A) Plastic steps	135	355	____
	(B) Sheet-metal steps	135	380	____
(21552/21556)	See 490/492			
(21560)	See 497			
21561	New Haven PA, *57-58*			
	(A) Plastic steps	125	340	____
	(B) One-rivet metal steps	125	350	____
(21570)	See 499			
(21571)	See 499			
21573	New Haven GE Electric, *58-59*	140	475	____
21720	Santa Fe PB, *58 u*	275	1150	____
(21800)	See 355			
21801	CNW Baldwin, *57-58*			
	(A) Unpainted	42	160	____
	(B) Painted	70	215	____
21801-1	CNW Baldwin, *58 u*			
	(A) Unpainted	70	215	____
	(B) Painted	85	245	____
21808	CNW Baldwin, *58 u*	50	155	____
(21)812	Texas & Pacific Baldwin, *59-60*	70	205	____
21813	M&StL Baldwin, *58 u, 60 u*	190	560	____
(21820)	See 372			
(21821)	See 372			
21831	Texas & Pacific GP-7, *58*			
	(A) "American Flyer Lines"	150	415	____
	(B) "Texas & Pacific"	185	590	____
21910/21910-1/21910-2 SF PA/PB/PA, *57-58*		370	940	____
21918/21918-1 Seaboard Baldwin, *58*		320	830	____
21920/21920-1 MP, PA/PA, *58**		340	1200	____
21920	MP, PA, *63-64*	160	660	____
21922/21922-1 MP, PA/PA, *59-60*		275	910	____
21925/21925-1 UP, PA/PA, *59-60**		235	900	____
21927	Santa Fe PA, *60-62*	110	250	____
22004	40-watt Transformer, *59-64*	2	9	____
22006	25-watt Transformer, *63*	2	9	____
22020	50-watt Transformer, *57-64*	1.50	5	____
22030	100-watt Transformer, *57-64*	4	16	____
22033	25-watt Transformer, *65*	1.50	4	____
22034	110-watt Transformer, *65*	4	13	____
22035	175-watt Transformer, *57-64*	17	75	____
22040	110-watt Transformer, *57-58*	5	18	____
22050	175-watt Transformer, *57-58*	12	39	____
22060	175-watt Transformer, *57-58*	12	39	____

		Good	Exc	Cond/$
22080	300-watt Transformer, *57-58*	34	130	____
22090	350-watt Transformer, *59-64*	50	185	____
23021	Imitation Grass, *57-59*	6	22	____
23022	Scenery Gravel, *57-59*	6	22	____
23023	Imitation Coal, *57-59*	5	13	____
23024	Rainbow Wire, *57-64*	4	10	____
23025	Smoke Cartridges, *57-59*	4	11	____
23026	Service Kit, *59-64*	6	24	____
23027	Track Cleaning Fluid, *57-59*	1.50	4	____
23028	Smoke Fluid Dispenser, *60-64*	1.50	5	____
23032	Equipment Kit, *60-61*	33	95	____
23036	Money Saver Kit, *60, 62, 64*	32	105	____
23040	Mountain, Tunnel, and Pass set, *58*		NRS	____
23249	Tunnel, *57-64*	9	42	____
23320	AF Traffic Master, *60*		NM	____
23561	Billboard Horn, *57-59*	9	44	____
23568	Whistling Billboard, *57-64*	10	50	____
23571	Truss Bridge, *57-64*	7	26	____
23581	Girder Bridge, *57-64*	8	32	____
23586	Wayside Station, *57-59*	25	105	____
23589	Passenger and Freight Station, *59 u*	15	47	____
23590	Control Tower, *57-59*	20	75	____
23596	Water Tank, *57-58*	25	90	____
23598	Talking Station Record, *57-59*	5	19	____
23599	Talking Station Record, *57*	9	36	____
23600	Crossing Gate w/ bell, *57-58*	13	80	____
23601	Crossing Gate, *59-62*	13	60	____
23602	Crossing Gate, *63-64*	13	60	____
(23)743	Track Maintenance Car			
23743	Track Maintenance Car, *60-64*	90	165	____
23750	Trestle Bridge, *57-61*	26	75	____
23758	Sam the Semaphore Man, *57*	29	85	____
23759	Bell Danger Signal, *56-60*	12	55	____
23760	Highway Flasher, *57-60*	9	38	____
23761	Semaphore, *57-60*	22	65	____
23763	Bell Danger Signal, *61-64*	11	55	____
23764	Flasher Signal, *61-64*	12	33	____
23769	Aircraft Beacon, *57-64*	13	65	____
23771	Stockyard and Car, *57-61*	29	120	____
23772	Water Tower, *57-64*	20	130	____
23774	Floodlight Tower, *57-64*	16	55	____
23778	Street Lamp set, *57-64*	8	31	____
23779	Oil Drum Loader, *57-61*	46	155	____
23780	Gabe the Lamplighter, *58-59*			
	(A) Plastic shed		NM	____
	(B) Metal shed	305	1050	____
23785	Coal Loader, *57-60*	130	340	____
23786	Talking Station, *57-59*	60	140	____

		Good	Exc	Cond/$
23787	Log Loader, *57-60*	80	275	____
23788	Suburban Station, *57-64*	10	60	____
23789	Station and Baggage Smasher, *58-59*	55	220	____
23791	Cow-on-Track, *57-59*	26	115	____
23796	Sawmill, *57-64*	90	260	____
23830	Piggyback Unloader, *59-60*	37	150	____
24003	Santa Fe Boxcar, *58*			
	(A) Unpainted	14	48	____
	(B) Painted			
24006	Great Northern Boxcar, *57-58*		NRS	____
24016	MKT Boxcar, *58*	225	930	____
24019	Seaboard Boxcar, *58 u*	18	48	____
(24022)	See 980			
24023	Baltimore & Ohio Boxcar, *58-59*	34	165	____
(24025)	See 981			
24026	Central of Georgia Boxcar, *58*	32	170	____
24029	BAR Boxcar, *57-60*	36	145	____
24030	MKT Boxcar, *60 u*			
	(A) Unpainted yellow plastic	10	31	____
	(B) Yellow-painted plastic		105	____
24033	Missouri Pacific Boxcar, *58*	50	150	____
24035	See 984			
24036	New Haven Boxcar, *58-60*	24	85	____
24039	Rio Grande Boxcar, *59*	9	50	____
24042	See 985			
24043	Boston & Maine Boxcar, *58-60*	33	115	____
24045	MEC Boxcar		NRS	____
24047	Great Northern Boxcar, *59*	50	255	____
24048	M&StL Boxcar, *59-62*	45	135	____
24052	UFGE Boxcar, *61*	11	23	____
24054	Santa Fe Boxcar, *62-64, 66*			
	(A) Red-painted plastic, *62-64*	20	55	____
	(B) Red unpainted plastic, *66*	9	46	____
(240)55	The Gold Belt Line Boxcar, *60-61*			
	(A) Opening w/ door	14	55	____
	(B) Opening w/o door	14	46	____
24056	Boston & Maine Boxcar, *61*			
	(A) Blue-painted black plastic	70	285	____
	(B) Unpainted blue plastic	27	130	____
24057	Mounds Boxcar, *62*			
	(A) White	5	19	____
	(B) Ivory	9	25	____
24058	Post Boxcar, *63-64*			
	(A) "Cereal"	8	18	____
	(B) "Cereals"	11	27	____
24059	Boston & Maine Boxcar, *63*	48	180	____
24060	M&StL Boxcar, *63-64*	39	145	____

		Good	Exc	Cond/$
24065	NYC Boxcar, *60-64*			
	(A) Knuckle couplers	41	110	____
	(B) Pike Master couplers	30	85	____
24066	L&N Boxcar, *60*			
	(A) Black plastic body	75	200	____
	(B) White plastic body	90	210	____
(24067)	Keystone Line Boxcar, *60 u**	1350	2250	____
24068	Planters Peanuts Boxcar, *61 u**		NRS	____
(24072)	See 929			
(24075)	See 994			
24076	Union Pacific Stock Car (mv), *57-60*			
	(A) w/ knuckle couplers	26	80	____
	(B) w/ Pike Master couplers	20	60	____
24077	Northern Pacific Stock Car, *59-62*			
	(A) Knuckle couplers	85	250	____
	(B) Pike Master couplers	60	205	____
24103	Norfolk & Western Gondola, *58, 63-64*			
	(A) Black plastic	7	24	____
	(B) Brown plastic		NRS	____
24106	Pennsylvania Gondola, *60 u*			
	(A) Unpainted	7	19	____
	(B) Painted	22	85	____
(24108)	See 911			
24109	C&O Gondola, *57-60*			
	(A) Silver plastic or cardboard pipes	18	55	____
	(B) Brown plastic pipes	33	115	____
	(C) Orange cardboard pipes	24	70	____
24110	Pennsylvania Gondola, *59 u*	5	15	____
(24112)	See 916			
24113	Delaware & Hudson Gondola, *57-59*	12	48	____
(24115)	See 920			
24116	Southern Gondola, *57-60*	12	60	____
24120	Texas & Pacific Gondola, *60*	14	65	____
(24122)	See 941			
24124	Boston & Maine Gondola, *63-64*			
	(A) Unpainted blue	5	19	____
	(B) Dark blue-painted	39	150	____
24125	Bethlehem Steel Gondola, *60-64*			
	(A) Gray-painted	22	80	____
	(B) Unpainted gray	9	19	____
24126	Frisco Gondola, *61*	33	115	____
24127	Monon Gondola, *61-65*			
	(A) Knuckle couplers	5	15	____
	(B) Pike Master couplers	4	14	____
(24130)	Pennsylvania Gondola, *60 u*			
	(A) Pike Master couplers	9	23	____
	(B) Fixed or Operating knuckles	4	16	____

		Good	Exc	Cond/$
24203	Baltimore & Ohio Hopper, *58, 63-64*			
	(A) Unpainted, *58*	11	34	____
	(B) Black-painted, *58*		NRS	____
	(C) PM trucks and couplers, *63-64*	15	55	____
(24205)	See 921			
24206	CB&Q Hopper, *58*	32	110	____
(24208)	See 924			
24209	CRP Hopper, *57-60*	27	85	____
24213	Wabash Hopper, *58-60*	13	47	____
24216	Union Pacific Hopper, *58-60*	22	85	____
24219	West. Maryland Hopper, *58-59*	31	130	____
24221	C&EI Hopper, *59-60*	35	155	____
24222	Domino Sugars Hopper, *63-64* *	150	460	____
24225	Santa Fe Hopper, *60-65*	10	50	____
24230	Peabody Hopper, *61-64*			
	(A) Knuckle couplers	21	90	____
	(B) Pike Master couplers	12	55	____
(24305)	See 912			
24309	Gulf Tank Car, *57-58*	4	25	____
24310	Gulf Tank Car, *58-60*	5	22	____
(24312)	See 926			
24313	Gulf Tank Car, *57-60*	21	80	____
24316	Mobilgas Tank Car, *57-61, 65-66*			
	(A) Knuckle couplers	14	45	____
	(B) Pike Master couplers	4	26	____
24319	PRR Salt Tank Car, *58* *	155	610	____
24320	Deep Rock Tank Car, *60*	125	480	____
24321	Deep Rock Tank Car, *59*	16	90	____
24322	Gulf Tank Car, *59*	15	75	____
24323	Baker's Chocolate Tank Car, *59-60* *			
	(A) Type II frame white w/ white ends	445	1900	____
	(B) Type II frame white w/ gray-painted ends	85	320	____
	(C) Type III frame white w/ open-bottom tank		NRS	____
24324	Hooker Tank Car, *59-60*	28	125	____
24325	Gulf Tank Car, *60*			
	(A) Type II plastic frame	6	20	____
	(B) Type III plastic frame	15	60	____
24328	Shell Tank Car, *62-66*	7	21	____
24329	Hooker Tank Car, *61, 63-66*	10	29	____
(24329)	Hooker Tank Car, *65-66 u*	9	36	____
24330	Baker's Chocolate Tank Car, *61-62*	27	100	____
24403	Illinois Central Reefer, *u* *			
	(A) Unpainted	13	25	____
	(B) Orange-painted		230	____
24409	Northern Pacific Reefer, *58*	310	1100	____
24413	ART Co. Reefer, *57-60*	38	135	____
24416	NW Reefer, *58*	680	1900	____

		Good	Exc	Cond/$
24419	Canadian National Reefer, *58-59*	95	400	____
(24420)	Simmons Reefer, *58* * *u*	660	940	____
24422	Great Northern Boxcars, *63-65, 66 u*	50	140	____
24422	Great Northern Reefers, *63-65, 66 u*			
	(A) Unpainted green plastic, non-opening door	12	23	____
	(B) Green-painted plastic, opening door	65	205	____
	(C) Green-painted plastic, non-opening door	60	195	____
24425	BAR Reefer, *60*	175	650	____
24426	Rath Packing Co. Reefer, *60-61*	170	610	____
24515	See 928, *N/A*			
24516	New Haven Flatcar, *57-59*	12	38	____
(24518)	See 936 Pennsylvania			
24519	Pennsylvania Flatcar, *58*	230	900	____
(24522)	See 944			
(24525)	See 945			
(24529)	Erie Floodlight, *57-58*	10	55	____
24533	American Flyer Lines Flatcar, *58-66*	9	39	____
(24535)	See 956			
24536	Monon Flatcar, *58*	385	1150	____
24537	New Haven Flatcar, *58 u*	10	49	____
24539	New Haven Flatcar, *58-59, 63-64*			
	(A) Silver plastic or cardboard pipes, *58-59*	12	43	____
	(B) Orange cardboard pipes, *63-64*	17	65	____
24540	New Haven Flatcar, *60 u*	47	220	____
24543	American Flyer Lines Crane, *58*	11	48	____
24546	AFL Work and Boom Car, *58-64*	10	42	____
24547	Erie Floodlight, *58*	245	720	____
24549	Erie Floodlight, *58-66*			
	(A) Yellow generator, knuckle couplers	15	44	____
	(B) Red generator	12	34	____
	(C) Yellow generator, PM couplers	8	27	____
24550	Monon Flatcar, *59-64*	23	85	____
24553	Rocket Transport Flatcar, *58-60*	22	85	____
24556	Rock Island Flatcar, *59*	22	95	____
24557	US Navy Flatcar, *59-61*	32	140	____
24558	Canadian Pacific Flatcar, *59-60*	75	360	____
24559	New Haven Flatcar, *59 u*	75	320	____
24561	American Flyer Lines Crane, *59-61*			
	(A) Gray-painted frame, knuckle couplers, *59*	10	42	____
	(B) Gray unpainted frame, Pike Master couplers, *60-61*	8	27	____
24562	New York Central Flatcar, *60*	14	44	____
(24564)	New Haven Flatcar, *60 u*	9	39	____
(245)65	FY&PRR Flatcar, *60-61* *	38	160	____
24566	New Haven Flatcar, *61-64*			
	(A) Black unpainted body	27	95	____
	(B) Gray unpainted body, *61*	300	980	____
24566	National Car Co. Flatcar, *61-65*	26	80	____

		Good	Exc	Cond/$
24569	AFL Crane, *62-66*	11	27	____
24572	US Navy Flatcar, *61*	38	155	____
24574	US Air Force Flatcar, *60-61*			
	(A) Knuckle couplers	40	200	____
	(B) Pike Master couplers	39	170	____
24575	National Car Co. Flatcar, *60-66*	17	65	____
(24575)	Unmarked Borden's Milk Flatcar, *66 u*	9	39	____
24577	Illinois Central Flatcar, *60-61, 63-64*			
	(A) Pike Master couplers	42	160	____
	(B) Knuckle couplers	45	150	____
24578	New Haven Flatcar, *62-63*	90	325	____
24579	Illinois Central Flatcar, *60-61*	45	200	____
24603	AFL Caboose, *57-58*	5	12	____
(24608)	See 930			
24610	AFL Caboose, *56-60 u*	5	10	____
(24618)	See 935			
24619	AFL Bay Window Caboose, *58*	20	95	____
24626	AFL Caboose, *58*	9	30	____
24627	AFL Caboose, *59-60*	4	11	____
24630	AFL Caboose, *56-61 u*	4	12	____
24631	American Flyer Lines Caboose, *59-61, 63-65*	8	34	____
24632	American Flyer Lines Caboose, *59*	28	85	____
24633	AFL Bay Window Caboose, *59-62*	19	85	____
24634	AFL Bay Window Caboose, *63-66*	20	60	____
24636	American Flyer Lines Caboose, *61-66*			
	(A) Red	6	15	____
	(B) Yellow-painted	150	520	____
	(C) Red-painted		NRS	____
24638	AFL Bay Window Caboose, *62*	27	95	____
(24702)	See 901			
(24705)	See 900			
(24708)	See 902			
(24712)	See 903			
(247)20	FY&PRR Coach, *59-61*			
	(A) Unpainted yellow	18	50	____
	(B) Yellow-painted	29	80	____
(247)30	FY&PRR Overland Exp. Baggage Car, *59-60*			
	(A) Unpainted yellow	20	55	____
	(B) Yellow-painted	29	80	____
24733	AFL Pikes Peak Coach, *57*	145	470	____
24739	AFL Niagara Falls Combination, *57*		NRS	____
(247)40	Baggage Express Combination, *60*	18	50	____
(247)50	FY&PRR Combination, *60-61*	50	180	____
(24772)	See 960			
24773	AFL Columbus Combination Car, *57-58, 60-62*	65	195	____
(24775)	See 960			
24776	AFL Columbus Combination Car, *59*	60	180	____

		Good	Exc	Cond/$
(24792)	See 961			
24793	AFL Jefferson Passenger Car, *57-58, 60-62*	70	235	____
24794	AFL Jefferson Passenger Car, *59*		2000	____
(24795)	See 961			
24796	AFL Jefferson Pullman Car, *59*	60	180	____
(24812)	See 962			
24813	AFL Hamilton Vista Dome Car, *57-58, 60-62*	60	180	____
24816	AFL Hamilton Vista Dome Car, *59*	60	180	____
(24832)	See 963			
24833	AFL Washington Observation Car, *57-58, 60-62*	65	195	____
(24835)	See 963			
24836	AFL Washington Observation Car, *59*	60	170	____
24837	Union Pacific Combination Car, *59-60**	85	290	____
24838	Union Pacific Passenger Car, *59-60**	90	385	____
24839	Union Pacific Vista Dome Car, *59-60**	95	360	____
24840	Union Pacific Observation Car, *59-60**	95	350	____
24843	Northern Pacific Combination Car, *58*	90	280	____
24846	Northern Pacific Passenger Car, *58*	90	280	____
24849	Northern Pacific Vista Dome Car, *58*	90	280	____
24853	Northern Pacific Observation Car, *58*	90	280	____
24856	MoPac Eagle Hill Combination Car, *58, 63-64**	125	395	____
24859	MoPac Eagle Lake Passenger Car, *58, 63-64**	130	495	____
24863	MoPac Eagle Creek Passenger Car, *58, 63-64**	120	475	____
24866	MoPac Eagle Valley Observation Car, *58, 63-64**	120	475	____
24867	AFL Combination Car, *58 u, 60 u*	46	175	____
24868	AFL Observation Car, *58 u, 60 u*	50	190	____
24869	AFL Passenger Car, *58 u, 60 u*	50	190	____
24963	Car Assortment, *58*		NRS	____
25003	American Flyer Flatcar, *57-60*	95	405	____
25005	Mail Car, *57*		NRS	____
25006	See 918			
(25007)	See 919			
(25012)	See 970			
(25015)	See 971			
25016	Southern Pacific Flatcar, *57-60*	44	155	____
25018	See 973			
25019	Operating Milk Car, *57-60*	65	185	____
25025	CB&Q Dump Car, *58-60*	80	255	____
25031	AFL Caboose, *58*		NRS	____
(25032)	See 915			
(25033)	See 915			
(25035)	See 979			
25036	See 979			

Good | Exc | Cond/$

		Good	Exc	Cond/$
(25039)	See 978			
25042	Erie Operating Boxcar, 58	70	215	
(25044)	See 969			
25045	Rocket Launcher Flatcar, 57-60	16	80	
25046	Rocket Launcher Flatcar, 60	14	85	
25049	Rio Grande Boxcar, 58-60	85	305	
25052	AFL Bay Window Caboose, 58	49	195	
(25056)	USM and Rocket Launcher set Operating Boxcar and Flatcar, 59	125	480	
25057	TNT Exploding Boxcar, 60	60	260	
25058	Southern Pacific Flatcar, 61-64	48	170	
25059	Rocket Launcher Flatcar, 60-64	21	90	
25060	CB&Q Hopper Dump Car, 61-64	80	300	
25061	TNT Exploding Boxcar, 61	95	340	
25062	Mine Carrier Exploding Boxcar, 62-64	125	450	
25071	AF Tie Car Flatcar, 61-64	7	35	
25081	NYC Operating Boxcar, 61-64	13	50	
25082	New Haven Operating Boxcar, 61-64	11	50	
25515	USAF Flatcar, 60-63	55	225	
26101	Curved Track Panel, 65-66	2.50	13	
26121	Straight Track Panel, 65-66	4	14	
26122	Straight Panel w/ whistle, 65-66	6	31	
26141	Right Switch Panel, 65-66	7	22	
26142	Left Switch Panel, 65-66	7	22	
26151	Crossover Panel, 65-66	7	16	
26300	PM Straight Track, 61-64	0.10	0.45	
26301	PM Straight Track, 61-64	0.10	0.45	
26302	PM Straight Track w/ uncoupler, 61-64	0.45	2.50	
26310	PM Curved Track, 61-64	0.10	0.45	
26320	PM RH Remote Switch, 61-64	7	13	
26321	PM LH Remote Switch, 61-64	8	14	
26322	PM 90° Crossing, 61-64	0.85	2.50	
26323	PM RH Manual Switch, 61-64	1.50	5	
26324	PM LH Manual Switch, 61-64	1.50	5	
26340	PM Steel Track Pins, 61-64	0.35	0.70	
26341	PM Insulating Pins, 61-64	0.35	0.70	
26342	PM Adapter Pins, 61-64	0.30	0.55	
26343	PM Track Locks, 61-64	0.30	0.55	
26344	PM Track Terminal, 61-64	0.20	0.35	
26415	Track Assortment, 60, 62		NRS	
26419	Accessory Package, u	4	15	
26425	Track Assortment Pack, 60	6	11	
26428	Accessory Pack, 58 u		NRS	
26520	Knuckle Coupler Kit, 57-64	0.85	4	
26521	Knuckle Coupler Kit, 57-58	NRS	12	
26601	Fiber Roadbed, 59-62	0.15	0.65	
26602	Fiber Roadbed, 59, 61-62	0.15	0.65	
26670	Track Trip, 57-58	4	14	

		Good	Exc	Cond/$
26671	Track Trip, *59*	3	10	____
26672	Track Trip, *60*	2	8	____
26673	Track Trip, *61-64*	2	7	____
26690	Track Terminal, w/ envelope, *57-59*	0.50	2	____
26691	Steel Pins, *57-60, 64*	0.45	0.90	____
26692	Fiber Pins, *57-60, 64*	0.45	0.90	____
26693	Track Locks, dz., *57-60, 64*	2	6	____
26700	Straight Track, *57-64*	0.15	0.65	____
26704	Manual uncoupler, u	0.45	0.90	____
26708	Horn Control, *57-58*	4	9	____
26710	Straight Track, *57-64*	0.15	0.65	____
26718	RC Switch, LH, *57*	6	13	____
26719	RC Switch, RH, *57*	6	13	____
26720	Curved Track, *57-64*	0.15	0.55	____
26722	Curved Track, dz.	6	11	____
26726	Straight Rubber Roadbed, half section, *58*	1	2	____
26727	Rubber Roadbed, half section, *58*	1	2	____
26730	Curved Track, half section, *57-64*	0.15	0.30	____
26739	Whistle Control, *57-58*	13	40	____
26742	RC Switches, pair, *57*	9	42	____
26744	Manual Switches, pair, *57-58*	4	16	____
26745	Railroad Crossing, *57-64*	1	8	____
26746	Rubber Roadbed, *57-64*	0.50	1.50	____
26747	Rubber Roadbed, *57-64*	0.50	1.50	____
26748	Re-railer, *57-64*	2.50	17	____
26749	Bumper, *57-60*	2	13	____
26751	Pike Planning Kit, *57-59*	8	24	____
26752	RC Uncoupler, *57-58, 60-61*	0.85	4	____
26756	Bumper, *61-64*	5	18	____
26760	RC Switches, pair, *58-64*	11	36	____
26761	RC Switch, LH, *58-64*	7	14	____
26762	RC Switch, RH, *58-64*	7	14	____
26770	Manual Switches, pair, *59-64*	4	14	____
26781	Trestle set, *57*	10	24	____
26782	Trestle set, *58-60*	4	16	____
26783	Hi-Trestles, *57*	8	20	____
26790	Trestle set, *61-64*	13	22	____
26810	Pow-R-Clips, *60-64*	0.20	0.40	____
27443	Lamps	0.85	2.50	____
27460	Lamp Assortment, *59, 64*	10	24	____

		New	Cond/$
0101	See (48712)		
390	See (48472)		
477/478	See (48126/48127)		
479	See (48129)		
480	See (48128)		
491	See (48476)		
591	See (48475)		
625	See (48405)		
0700	NASG Boxcar, *81 u*	120	___
792	See (48478)		
804-A/804-D	See (48120/48121)		
893	See (48481)		
960	See (48938)		
961	See (48939)		
962	See (48942)		
963	See (48940)		
993	See (48480)		
1094	See (48485)		
1194	See (48486)		
1225	See (48016)		
1261	See (48492)		
1295	See (48494)		
1395	See (48493)		
1496	See (52094)		
1596	See (52095)		
1946-1996	See (48324)		
1990	See (48473)		
1994	See (48487)		
1995	See (48491)		
(2300)	Oil Drum Loader, *83-87*	140	___
(2321)	Operating Sawmill, *84, 86-87*	125	___
3993	See (48482)		
5600	See (48013)		
6001/6002	See (48124/48125)		
8000	See (4)8000		
8001	See (4)8001		
8002	See (4)8002		
8005	See (4)8005		
8007	See (4)8007		
8008	See (4)8008		
8009	See (4)8009		
8010	See (4)8010		
8014	See (4)8014		
8100/8101	See (4)8100/(4)8101		
8102/8103	See (4)8102/(4)8103		
8104/8105	See (4)8104/(4)8105		
8106/8107	See (4)8106/(4)8107		
8112/8113	See (4)8112/(4)8113		
8114/8115/8116	See (4)8114/(4)8115/(4)8116		
8117	See (4)8117		
8118	See (4)8118		

		New	Cond/$
8119	See (4)8119		
8123	See (4)8123		
8150/8152	Southern Pacific Alco PA-1 AA set, *81*	350	____
8151	Southern Pacific Alco PA-1 B Unit, *82*	175	____
8153/8155	Baltimore & Ohio Alco PA-1 AA set (HARR#1), *81, 83*	305	____
(8154)	Baltimore & Ohio Alco PA-1 B Unit (HARR#1), *81, 83*	115	____
8200	See (4)8200		
8201	See (4)8201		
8251/8253	Erie Alco PA-1 AA set, *82*	245	____
8252	Erie Alco PA-1 B Unit, *82*	120	____
8308	See (4)8308		
8309	See (4)8309		
8310	See (4)8310		
8311	See (4)8311		
8312	See (4)8312		
8313	See (4)8313		
8314	See (4)8314		
8318	See (4)8318		
8319	See (4)8319		
8321	See (4)8321		
8350	Boston & Maine GP-7 (HARR#2), *83*	350	____
8403	See (4)8403		
8458	Southern GP-9 (HARR#3), *84*	225	____
8459	Chessie System GP-20, *84*	275	____
8460	See (48004)		
8505	See (4)8505		
8551	Santa Fe GP-20, *86*	210	____
8552	New York Central GP-9 (HARR#4), *86*	190	____
8553	See (48003)		
8609	See (4)8609		
8651	See 8551, *N/A*		
8681	See (48405)		
8706	See (4)8706		
8707	See (4)8707		
8711	See (4)8711		
8805	See (4)8805		
8806	See (4)8806		
8904	See (4)8904		
8905	See (4)8905		
8906	See (4)8906		
8907	See (4)8907		
8908	See (4)8908		
8909	See (4)8909		
8910	See (4)8910		
8911	See (4)8911		
8912	See (4)8912		
8913	See (4)8913		
8914	See (4)8914		
8915	See (4)8915		

		New	Cond/S
8920	See (4)8920		
8921	See (4)8921		
8922	See (4)8922		
8923	See (4)8923		
8924	See (4)8924		
8925	See (4)8925		
8933	See (4)8933		
8934	See (4)8934		
8941	See (4)8941		
9000	B&O Flatcar w/ trailers (HARR#1), *81, 83*	35	_____
9001	See (4)9001		
9002	B&M Flatcar w/ logs (HARR#2), *83*	80	____
9003	See (4)9003		
9004	Southern Flatcar w/ trailers (HARR#3), *84*	37	____
9005	NYC Flatcar w/ trailers (HARR#4), *86*	33	____
9100	Gulf 1-D Tank Car, *79*	55	____
9101	Union 76 1-D Tank Car, *80*	30	____
9102	B&O 1-D Tank Car (HARR#1), *81, 83*	24	____
9104	B&M 3-D Tank Car (HARR#2), *83*	90	____
9105	Southern 3-D Tank Car (HARR#3), *84*	25	____
9106	NYC 3-D Tank Car (HARR#4), *86*	26	____
9200	Chessie System Hopper w/ coal load, *79*	40	____
9201	B&O Covered Hopper (HARR#1), *81, 83*	30	____
9203	Boston & Maine Hopper (HARR#2), *83*	70	____
9204	Southern Hopper (HARR#3), *84*	24	____
9205	Pennsylvania Covered Hopper, *84*	35	____
9206	New York Central Covered Hopper, *84*	29	____
9207	B&O Covered Hopper, *86*	25	____
9208	Santa Fe Covered Hopper, *86*	24	____
9209	New York Central Hopper (HARR#4), *86*	24	____
9300	Burlington Gondola, *80*	19	____
9301	B&O Gondola w/ canisters (HARR#1), *81, 83*	22	____
9303	Southern Gondola w/ canisters (HARR#3), *84*	24	____
9304	NYC Gondola w/ canisters (HARR#4), *86*	22	____
9400	Chessie System B/W Caboose, *80*	25	____
9401	B&O B/W Caboose (HARR#1), *81, 83*	31	____
9402	B&M B/W Caboose (HARR#2), *83*	70	____
9403	Southern B/W Caboose (HARR#3), *84*	32	____
9404	NYC B/W Caboose (HARR#4), *86*	33	____
9405	Santa Fe B/W Caboose, *86*	33	____
(9500)	Southern Pacific Combination Car, *81*	90	____
(9501)	Southern Pacific Passenger Car, *81*	130	____
(9502)	Southern Pacific Vista Dome Car, *81*	130	____
(9503)	Southern Pacific Observation Car, *81*	90	____
9504	Erie Combination Car, *82*	50	____
9505	Erie Passenger Car, *82*	80	____
9506	Erie Vista Dome Car, *82*	75	____
9507	Erie Observation Car, *82*	50	____
9700	Santa Fe Boxcar, *79*		
	(A) w/ door nibs	95	____
	(B) w/o door nibs	65	____

		New	Cond/$
9701	Rock Island Boxcar, *80*	35	___
9702	Baltimore & Ohio "Sentinel" Boxcar (HARR#1), *81, 83*	42	___
9703	Boston & Maine Boxcar (HARR #2), *83*	90	___
9704	Southern Boxcar (HARR#3), *84*	35	___
9705	Pennsylvania Boxcar, *84*	55	___
9706	New York Central "Pacemaker" Boxcar, *84*	75	___
9707	Railbox Boxcar, *84*	55	___
9708	Conrail Boxcar, *84*	40	___
9709	Baltimore & Ohio Boxcar, *86*	29	___
9710	Santa Fe Boxcar, *86*	30	___
9711	Southern Pacific Boxcar, *86*	28	___
9712	Illinois Central Gulf Boxcar, *86*	31	___
9713	New York Central Boxcar (HARR#4), *86*	40	___
11492	See (48477)		
20602	See (48479)		
21503	See (48710)		
22997	Oil Drum Loader, *99*	160	___
24063	See (48489)		
24319	See (48402)		
29425	See (48316)		
29426	See (48317)		
31337	See (48498)		
(32921)	See 49807		
(4)8000	Southern Pacific GP-9 "8000" (HARR#5), *87*	190	___
(4)8001	Illinois Central Gulf GP-20 "8001", *87*	200	___
(4)8002	Southern Pacific GP-9 Dummy "8002" (HARR#5), *88*	135	___
(48003)	Santa Fe GP-20 Dummy "8553", *88*	140	___
(48004)	Chessie System GP-20 Dummy "8460", *88*	160	___
(4)8005	Pennsylvania GP-9 "8005", *89*	185	___
(4)8007	Burlington Northern GP-20 "8007", *90*	315	___
(4)8008	New Haven EP-5 "8008", *91*	225	___
(4)8009	American Flyer GM GP-7 "8009", *91*	170	___
(4)8010	Milwaukee Road EP-5 "8010", *92*	195	___
(48013)	Conrail GP-7 "5600", *05*	195	___
(4)8014	Northern Pacific GP-9 "8014", *95*	210	___
(48016)	Merry Christmas GP-20 "1225", *95*	180	___
(48017)	Nickel Plate Road GP-9 set "496/497", *97*	275	___
(48019)	SP GP-20, "4060", *98*	175	___
(48020)	Milwaukee Road GP-9, "304", *98*	200	___
(48021)	Conrail SD-40-2 decorated "6381", *98*	NM	___
(48022)	Conrail SD-40-2 undecorated, *98*	NM	___
(48023)	Santa Fe Merger GP-9 "2927", *99*	250	___
(48033)	Rock Island GP9 Road Diesel "1272", *02*	250	___
(48034)	Seaboard Baldwin Diesel Switcher "1413", *03*	250	___
(48035)	Santa Fe Baldwin Diesel Switcher "2257", *03*	250	___
(48036)	NYC USRA Light Mikado, *03*	600	___
(4)8100/(4)8101	Wabash Alco PA-1 AA set "8100/8101" (HARR#6), *88*	245	___
(4)8102/(4)8103	C&O Alco PA-1 AA set "8102/8103" (HARR#7), *89*	215	___

		New	Cond/$
(4)8104/(4)8105	American Flyer RailScope Alco PA-1 AA set "8104/8105", *89-90*	NM	____
(4)8106/(4)8107	UP Alco PA-1 AA set "8106/8107" (HARR#8), *90*	280	____
(4)8112/(4)8113	MoPac Alco PA-1 AA set "8112/8113", *91*	270	____
(4)8114/(4)8115/(4)8116	NP Alco PA-1 ABA set "8114/8115/8116", *92*	330	____
(4)8117	NP Alco PA-1 B Unit w/ RailSounds "8117", *92*	105	____
(4)8118	MoPac Alco PA-1 B Unit w/ RailSounds "8118", *92 u*	100	____
(4)8119	UP Alco PA-1 B Unit w/ RailSounds "8119" (HARR#8), *92 u*	105	____
(48120/48121)	WP Alco PA-1 AA set "804-A/804-D", *93*	225	____
(48122)	WP Alco PA-1 B Unit w/ RailSounds, *93*	115	____
(4)8123	SP Alco PA-1 B Unit w/ RailSounds "8123", *93*	125	____
(48124/48125)	D&RGW Alco PA-1 AA set "6001/6002", *94*	NM	____
(48126/48127)	Silver Flash Alco PA-1 AB set "477/478", *95*	285	____
(48128)	Silver Flash Alco PA-1 B Unit "480", *95*	85	____
(48129)	Silver Flash Alco PA-1 A Unit Dummy "479", *96*	85	____
(48130)	SF Alco PA-1/PB-1 Diesel Locomotives "51-52", *97*	275	____
(48135)	NYC Alco PA B Unit "4302", *03*	150	____
(48200)	TCA AT&SF Boxcar, *97*	85	____
(4)8200	Wabash 4-6-4 "8200" (HARR#6), *88*	100	____
(4)8201	Santa Fe 4-6-4 "8201", *88*	NM	____
(48203)	TTOS NYC Reefer, *97*	60	____
(48204)	TCA D&RGW Boxcar, *97*	70	____
(48205)	NASG Pacific Fruit Express Reefer, *97*	45	____
(48208)	TCA New England Hopper, *98*	50	____
(48209)	TTOS Cotton Belt Boxcar, *98*	70	____
(48210)	TCA New England Hopper, *98*	45	____
(48211)	NASG Magnolia Tank Car, *98*	50	____
(48212)	TTOS SP Tank Car, *N/A*	NRS	____
(48213)	TCA L&N Boxcar, *99 u*	75	____
(48214)	NASG GN Caboose, *99 u*	85	____
48215	Monsanto Hopper, *99 u*	85	____
(48217)	TTOS SP Gondola, *00*	100	____
(48218)	TTOS SP Crane Car, *00*	100	____
48219	TCA Ship It on the Frisco Boxcar, *01 u*	65	____
(48220)	NASG Deep Rock Tank Car, *00 u*	100	____
(48221)	Norfolk Southern 2-bay Hopper, *01*	60	____
(48222)	TTOS British Columbia Tank Car, *00*	65	____
(48223)	TCA National Toy Train Museum Tank Car	60	____
(48224)	NASG Gulf Tank Car, *01*	75	____
(48225)	TTOS San Diego Boxcar, *02u*	CP	____
(48226)	Toy Train Museum Flatcar w/ Wheel Load, *02u*	CP	____
(48227)	TTOS D&S Operating Hopper, *02u*	CP	____
(48228)	NASG Cook Paint Tank Car, *02u*	CP	____
(48230)	Toy Train Museum Gondola w/ Pipe Load, *03u*	CP	____
48300	Southern Pacific "Overnight" Boxcar (HARR#5), *87*	35	____
48301	D&RGW Boxcar, *87*	34	____
48302	Canadian Pacific Boxcar, *87*	33	____

		New	Cond/$
48303	Chessie System Boxcar, *87*	38	___
48304	Burlington Northern Boxcar, *87*	41	___
48305	Wabash Boxcar (HARR#6), *88*	28	___
48306	Seaboard Coast Line Boxcar, *88*	30	___
48307	Western Pacific Boxcar, *88*	34	___
(4)8308	Maine Central Boxcar "8308", *90*	75	___
(4)8309	Christmas Boxcar "8309", *90 u*	75	___
(4)8310	MKT Boxcar "8310", *91*	36	___
(4)8311	Christmas Boxcar "8311", *91 u*	65	___
(4)8312	Missouri Pacific Boxcar "8312", *92*	55	___
(4)8313	BAR "State of Maine" Boxcar "8313", *92*	55	___
(4)8314	Christmas Boxcar "8314", *92 u*	49	___
(48316)	Bangor & Aroostook Reefer "29425", *93*	43	___
(48317)	Rath Packing Reefer "29426", *93*	43	___
(4)8318	A.C. Gilbert Boxcar "8318", *93*	40	___
(4)8319	Christmas Boxcar "8319", *93*	40	___
48320	NKP Boxcar, *94*	34	___
(4)8321	Christmas Boxcar "8321", *94*	39	___
(48322)	New Haven Boxcar, *95*	38	___
(48323)	Christmas Boxcar, *95*	35	___
(48324)	AF 50th Anniversary Boxcar "1946-1996", *96*	38	___
(48325)	Holiday Boxcar, *96*	36	___
(48326)	TCA B&O Boxcar, *96*	65	___
(48327)	AF Christmas Boxcar "900", *97*	40	___
(48328)	GN Boxcar "900-197", *97*	40	___
(48329)	AT&SF Boxcar "900-297", map graphic, *97*	32	___
(48330)	PRR Boxcar "900-397", *97*	36	___
(48332)	MKT Boxcar, "937", *98*	33	___
(48333)	Bangor and Aroostook Boxcar, "982", *98*	50	___
(48334)	Seaboard Boxcar, "942", *98*	34	___
(48335)	Christmas 1998 Gondola, *98*	50	___
(48340)	American Flyer 2000 Christmas car, *00*	65	___
(48341)	American Flyer 1999 Christmas car, *99*	55	___
(48342)	American Flyer Christmas Boxcar, *01*	55	___
48343	Great Northern Boxcar, *01*	47	___
(48346)	Christmas Boxcar "2002", *02*	55	___
(48347)	C&O Boxcar "2701", *02*	55	___
(48348)	NP Boxcar "31226", *02*	55	___
(48349)	Goofy Boxcar, *03*	55	___
(48351)	Donald Duck Boxcar, *03*	55	___
(48353)	2003 American Flyer Christmas Boxcar, *03*	50	___
(48362)	Pennsylvania Boxcar "47133", *03*	50	___
48400	SP 3-D Tank Car (HARR #5), *87*	34	___
(48402)	Penn Salt 1-D Tank Car "24319", *92*	100	___
(4)8403	British Columbia 1-D Tank Car "8403", *93*	105	___
48404	US Army 1-D Tank Car, *94*	42	___
(48405)	Shell 1-D Tank Car "625" "8681", *95*	45	___
(48406)	Celanese Chemicals Tank Car, *96*	37	___
(48407)	Gilbert Chemicals Tank Car, *96*	39	___
(48408)	Sunoco 1-D Tank Car "625", *97*	45	___
(48410)	Tank Train 1-D Tank Car "44587", *99*	80	___
(48411)	Gilbert Chemicals Tank Car "48411", *02*	55	___

		New	Cond/$
(48412)	Alaska 3-D Tank Car, *02*	50	___
(48413)	Diamond Chemicals Tank Car "19418", *03*	50	___
(48436)	See (48476)		
(48470)	NASG Jersey Central Boxcar, *88 u*	105	___
(48471)	NASGMKT 1-D Tank Car "120089", *89 u*	220	___
(48472)	NASG Pennzoil 3-D Tank Car "390", *90 u*	145	___
[48473]	TCA Central of Georgia Boxcar "1990", *90 u*	65	___
(48474)	TCA CNW Reefer "70165", *91 u*	115	___
(48475)	NASG Boraxo Covered Hopper "591", *91 u*	70	___
(48476)	NASG NYC Reefer "491", *91 u*	70	___
(48477)	TCA Ralston-Purina Boxcar "11492", *92 u*	80	___
(48478)	NASG Burlington Boxcar "792", *92 u*	85	___
(48479)	NASG NKP Flatcar w/ Ertl trailer "20602", *92 u*	105	___
(48480)	NASG Susquehanna Boxcar "993", *93 u*	85	___
(48481)	NASG REA Reefer "893", *93 u*	60	___
(48482)	TCA Great Northern Boxcar "3993", *93 u*	90	___
(48483)	A.C. Gilbert Society "Boys Club" Boxcar, *93 u*	65	___
(48484)	A.C. Gilbert Society "Boys At The Gate" Boxcar, *93 u*	55	___
(48485)	NASG Northern Pacific Boxcar "1094", *94 u*	48	___
(48486)	NASG NYNH&H Boxcar "1194", *94 u*	48	___
(48487)	TCA Yorkrail Boxcar "1994", *94 u*	105	___
(48489)	TCA Penn Dutch Boxcar "91653", *97 u*	105	___
(48490)	TTOS Western Pacific Boxcar "101645", *95 u*	75	___
(48491)	TCA Burlington Northern Flatcar w/ trailers "1995", *95 u*	75	___
(48492)	TCA Northern Pacific Boxcar "1261", *95 u*	75	___
(48493)	NASG Southern Pacific TTUX Flatcars w/ trailers "1395", *95 u*	75	___
(48494)	NASG Lehigh Valley Covered Grain Hopper "1295", *95 u*	65	___
(48495)	St. Louis S Gaugers Monsanto 1-D Tank Car, white, *95 u*	85	___
(48496)	St. Louis S Gaugers Monsanto 1-D Tank Car, orange, *95 u*	480	___
(48497)	TCA MKT 3-D Tank Car "117018", *96 u*	90	___
(48498)	TTOS Western Pacific Boxcar "31337", *96 u*	80	___
48500	Southern Pacific Gondola w/ canisters (HARR#5), *87*	26	___
48501	Southern Pacific Flatcar w/ trailers (HARR#5), *87*	34	___
48502	Wabash Flatcar w/ trailers (HARR#6), *88*	34	___
48503	Wabash Gondola w/ canisters (HARR#6), *88*	22	___
(4)8505	Illinois Central Gulf Flatcar w/ bulkheads "8505", *90*	35	___
48507/48508	USArmy Flatcars w/ tanks (2), *95*	65	___
(48509)	AF Equipment Co. Flatcar w/ farm tractors, *95*	41	___
(48510)	Nickel Plate Road Gondola w/ canisters, *95*	30	___
(48511)	TTUX Triple Crown Flatcars w/ trailers, *96*	80	___
(48513)	CSX Flatcar w/ generator, *96*	30	___
(48514)	Intermodal TTUX Set, 2 cars, 2 trailers, *97*	75	___
(48515)	New Haven Flatcar, *99*	CP	___
(48516)	SP Searchlight Car "627", *97*	50	___

		New	Cond/$
(48524)	Borden's Flatcar, 01	50	___
(48525)	Burlington Gondola, 01	50	___
(48526)	Reading Gondola with Pipes "38708", 02	50	___
(48527)	Santa Fe Flat Car with Jet Rocket "90019", 02	50	___
(48528)	Conrail Flatcar w/ Wheel Loader, 02	60	___
(48529)	NYC Flatcar w/ Wheel Load, 02	50	___
48531	Chessie Flatcar with Cable Reel "48531", 03	60	___
(48532)	SP Flatcar with Trailers "513183", 03	50	___
48600	Southern Pacific Hopper (HARR#5), 87	29	___
48601	Union Pacific Covered Hopper, 87	28	___
48602	Erie Covered Hopper, 87	28	___
48603	Wabash Hopper w/ coal load (HARR#6), 88	28	___
48604	Milwaukee Road Covered Hopper, 88	29	___
48605	Burlington Northern Covered Hopper, 88	30	___
(48608)	Domino Sugar Covered Hopper "49608", 92	65	___
(4)8609	D&H Covered Hopper "8609", 93	37	___
48610	NKP Covered Hopper, 94	30	___
(48611)	Cargill Covered Grain Hopper, 95	37	___
(48612)	ADM 3-Bay Covered Hopper, 97	38	___
(48613)	B&LE Hoppers 4-pack, 98	130	___
(48614)	B&LE Hopper, 98	34	___
48619	Union Pacific Hopper, 01	50	___
(48620)	B&O Hopper "435350", 02	50	___
(48621)	CN Covered Hopper, 02	50	___
48622	Burlington Hopper "170616", 03	50	___
48700	SP B/W Caboose (HARR#5), 87	32	___
48701	Illinois Central Gulf B/W Caboose, 87	33	___
48702	Wabash S/W Caboose (HARR#6), 88	33	___
48703	Union Pacific S/W Caboose, 88	36	___
48705	Pennsylvania S/W Caboose, 89	38	___
(4)8706	BN S/W Caboose "8706", 90	42	___
(4)8707	NH S/W Caboose "8707", 91	33	___
(48710)	Conrail B/W Caboose "21503", 95	33	___
(4)8711	Northern Pacific B/W Caboose "8711", 95	40	___
(48712)	Happy New Year B/W Caboose "0101", 95	48	___
(48713)	Nickel Plate Road Caboose, 97	44	___
(48714)	SP S/W Caboose "990", 97	43	___
(48715)	Milwaukee Road Caboose, 97	50	___
(48718)	C&NW Caboose, 98	48	___
(48719)	Conrail B/W Caboose, "21137", 98	34	___
(48721)	Santa Fe Caboose "999628", 99	70	___
(48722)	Rock Island B/W Caboose "17778", 02	55	___
48723	Santa Fe Boom Car "206982", 03	50	___
48724	Seaboard S/W Caboose "49658", 03	50	___
48725	NYC Caboose, 03	50	___
48800	Wabash Reefer (HARR#6), 88	30	___
48801	Union Pacific Reefer, 88	29	___
48802	Pennsylvania Reefer, 88	36	___
(4)8805	National Dairy Despatch Insulated Boxcar "8805", 90	50	___
(4)8806	REA Reefer "8806", 94	34	___
(4)8807	NKP Reefer, 94	32	___

		New	Cond/$
48808	PFE Refrigerator Car "30000", *03*	50	___
48900	C&O Combination Car (HARR#7), *89*	47	___
48901	C&O Passenger Car (HARR#7), *89*	55	___
48902	C&O Vista Dome Car (HARR#7), *89*	50	___
48903	C&O Observation Car (HARR#7), *89*	47	___
(4)8904	UP Combination Car "8904" (HARR#8), *90*	43	___
(4)8905	UP Passenger Car "8905" (HARR#8), *90*	55	___
(4)8906	UP Vista Dome Car "8906" (HARR# 8), *90*	50	___
(4)8907	UP Observation Car "8907" (HARR#8), *90*	47	___
(4)8908	UP Passenger Car "8908" (HARR#8), *90 u*	90	___
(4)8909	UP Vista Dome Car "8909" (HARR#8), *90 u*	105	___
(4)8910	MoPac Combination Car "8910", *91*	47	___
(4)8911	MoPac Vista Dome Car "8911", *91*	47	___
(4)8912	MoPac Passenger Car "8912", *91*	47	___
(4)8913	MoPac Observation Car "8913", *91*	47	___
(4)8914	MoPac Passenger Car "8914", *91*	55	___
(4)8915	MoPac Vista Dome Car "8915", *91*	55	___
(4)8920	Northern Pacific Combination Car "8920", *92*	47	___
(4)8921	Northern Pacific Passenger Car "8921", *92*	47	___
(4)8922	Northern Pacific Vista Dome Car "8922", *92*	47	___
(4)8923	Northern Pacific Observation Car "8923", *92*	47	___
(4)8924	Northern Pacific Vista Dome Car "8924", *92*	47	___
(4)8925	Northern Pacific Passenger Car "8925", *92*	55	___
(48926)	WP "California Zephyr" Combination Car "CZ801", *93*	37	___
(48927)	WP "California Zephyr" Vista Dome Car "CZ814", *93*	40	___
(48928)	WP "California Zephyr" Vista Dome Car "CZ815", *93*	40	___
(48929)	WP "California Zephyr" Vista Dome Car "CZ813", *93*	42	___
(48930)	WP "California Zephyr" Vista Dome Car "CZ811", *93*	46	___
(48931)	WP "California Zephyr" Observation Car "CZ882", *93*	37	___
(48932)	WP "California Zephyr" Dining Car "CZ842", *93*	43	___
(4)8933	MoPac Dining Car "8933", *94*	40	___
(4)8934	Northern Pacific Dining Car "8934", *94*	43	___
(48935)	New Haven Combination Car, *95*	55	___
(48936)	New Haven Vista Dome Car, *95*	55	___
(48937)	New Haven Observation Car, *95*	55	___
(48938)	Silver Flash Combination Car "960", *95*	70	___
(48939)	Silver Flash Passenger Car "961", *95*	70	___
(48940)	Silver Flash Observation Car "963", *95*	70	___
(4)8941	Union Pacific Vista Dome Dining Car "8941", *95*	55	___
(48942)	Vista Dome Car "962", *96*	120	___
(48943)	New Haven Vista Dome Dining Car, *96*	55	___
(48944)	AT&SF "Super Chief" Passenger 4-pack "995-98", *97*	225	___
(48961)	NYC Streamlined Passenger Car 2-pack, *02*	140	___
48964	NYC Baggage Car "9149", *03*	60	___
48965	B&O Passenger Car 2-Pack, *03*	120	___

		New	Cond/$
(4)9001	NYC Searchlight Car "9001", *90*	37	___
(4)9003	Union Pacific Searchlight Car "9003", *91*	39	___
49006	Milwaukee Road Animated S/W Caboose, *92*	33	___
(49009)	AF Lines Flatcar w/ derrick, *96*	37	___
(49010)	Stable of Champions Horse Car, *96*	32	___
49011	UP "Moe & Joe" Animated Flatcar "15100", *03*	70	___
49012	Santa Fe Crane Car " 199707", *03*	70	___
(49600)	Union Pacific "Pony Express" set (HARR#8), *90*	700	___
(49601)	Missouri Pacific "Eagle" set, *91*	520	___
(49602)	Northern Pacific "North Coast Limited" set, *92*	740	___
(49604)	Western Pacific "California Zephyr" set, *93*	395	___
(49605)	New Haven Passenger Car set, *95*	170	___
(49606)	Silver Flash set, *95*	530	___
49608	See (48608)	60	___
(49611)	NYC Alco PA Passenger set, *02*	530	___
49612	B&O 4-Car Passenger set, *03*	800	___
(49805)	No. 23780 Gabe the Lamplighter, *01*	130	___
(49806)	No. 23796 Sawmill, *01*	100	___
(49807)	No. 752 Seaboard Coaler, *01*	175	___
(49809)	No. 772 Water Tower, *02*	90	___
49810	No. 787 Log Loader, *03*	130	___
49811	No. 773 Oil Derrick, *03*	60	___
49812	No. 755 Talking Station, *03*	200	___
49813	No. 789 Baggage Smasher, *03*	130	___
49814	No. 774 Floodlight Tower, *03*	100	___
(52094)	NASG Ann Arbor Covered Grain Hopper "1496", *96 u*	50	___
(52095)	NASG Mobil 1-D Tank Car "1596", *96 u*	70	___
70165	See (48474)		
91653	See (48489)		
101645	See (48490)		
117018	See (48497)		
120089	See (48471)		
CZ801	See (48926)		
CZ811	See (48930)		
CZ813	See (48929)		
CZ814	See (48927)		
CZ815	See (48928)		
CZ842	See (48932)		
CZ882	See (48931)		

FREE TRIAL ISSUE!

BUSINESS REPLY MAIL
FIRST-CLASS MAIL   PERMIT NO. 16   WAUKESHA, WI

POSTAGE WILL BE PAID BY ADDRESSEE

CLASSIC TOY TRAINS®

PO BOX 1612
WAUKESHA WI 53187-9950

AMERICAN MODELS
1981–2004

		Retail	Cond/$

Note: All locomotives are AC powered and ready to run unless noted otherwise.

		Retail	Cond/$
(100)	Undecorated 40' Boxcar	33.95	____
(102)	B&O 40' Boxcar	33.95	____
(105)	D&RGW 40' Boxcar	33.95	____
(112)	Soo 40' Boxcar	33.95	____
(113)	NYC 40' Boxcar	33.95	____
(114)	PRR 40' Boxcar	33.95	____
(115)	ATSF 40' Boxcar	33.95	____
(116)	SEA 40' Boxcar	33.95	____
(117)	SP 40' Boxcar	33.95	____
(118)	UP 40' Boxcar	33.95	____
(119)	C&O 40' Boxcar	33.95	____
(119B)	C&O 40' Boxcar	33.95	____
(121)	NYC Pacemaker 40' Boxcar	36.95	____
(122)	Rutland 40' Boxcar	36.95	____
(125)	P&LE 40' Boxcar	34.95	____
(126)	NP 40' Boxcar	34.95	____
(128)	NH 40' Boxcar	33.95	____
(129)	GN 40' Boxcar	33.95	____
(130)	GM&O 40' Boxcar	33.95	____
(131)	N&W 40' Boxcar	33.95	____
(132)	CP 40' Boxcar	33.95	____
(133)	M&StL 40' Boxcar	33.95	____
(134)	EL 40' Boxcar	33.95	____
(135)	SP 40' Boxcar	34.95	____
(136)	Susquehanna 40' Boxcar	33.95	____
(137)	C&NW 40' Boxcar	33.95	____
(138)	Conrail 40' Boxcar	33.95	____
(139)	Southern 40' Boxcar	33.95	____
(140)	MP 40' Boxcar	33.95	____
(141)	NYC 40' Boxcar	34.95	____
(142)	Rock Island 40' Boxcar	33.95	____
(175)	ICG 40' Boxcar "418388"	30.95	____
(176)	Reading 40' Boxcar "1104273"	30.95	____
(177)	ACY 40' Boxcar	30.95	____
(178)	BN 40' Boxcar "131589"	30.95	____
(179)	Burlington Route 40' Boxcar "62366"	30.95	____
(180R)	NP 40' Boxcar "19202"	30.95	____
(180G)	NP 40' Boxcar "19202"	30.95	____
(181)	NYC 40' Boxcar	39.95	____
(200)	Undecorated 2-bay Hopper, rib-sided	29.95	____
(201)	C&O 2-bay Hopper, rib-sided	29.95	____
(202)	WM 2-bay Hopper, rib-sided	29.95	____
(204)	Erie 2-bay Hopper, rib-sided	29.95	____
(205)	N&W 2-bay Hopper, rib-sided	29.95	____
(206)	NYC 2-bay Hopper, rib-sided	29.95	____
(207)	PRR 2-bay Hopper, rib-sided	29.95	____
(208)	PEAB 2-bay Hopper, rib-sided	29.95	____

		Retail	Cond/$
(209)	Southern 2-bay Hopper, rib-sided	29.95	____
(210)	UP 2-bay Hopper, rib-sided	29.95	____
(211)	SP 2-bay Hopper, rib-sided	29.95	____
(212)	D&RGW 2-bay Hopper, rib-sided	29.95	____
(213)	Virginian 2-bay Hopper, rib-sided	29.95	____
(214)	Reading 2-bay Hopper, rib-sided	29.95	____
(215)	CB&Q 2-bay Hopper, rib-sided	29.95	____
(216)	LV 2-bay Hopper, rib-sided	29.95	____
(217)	Interstate 2-bay Hopper, "INT 6012", rib-sided	29.95	____
(218)	BN 2-bay Hopper, rib-sided	29.95	____
(223)	Burlington Route Express 40' Plug Door Boxcar "79225"	30.95	____
(250)	Undecorated 2-bay Hopper, offset-sided	29.95	____
(251)	ATSF 2-bay Hopper, offset-sided	29.95	____
(252)	CP 2-bay Hopper, offset-sided	29.95	____
(253)	GN 2-bay Hopper, offset-sided	29.95	____
(254)	NP 2-bay Hopper, offset-sided	29.95	____
(255)	IC 2-bay Hopper, offset-sided	29.95	____
(256)	NYC 2-bay Hopper, offset-sided	29.95	____
(257)	L&N 2-bay Hopper, offset-sided	29.95	____
(258)	MILW 2-bay Hopper, offset-sided	29.95	____
(259)	UP 2-bay Hopper, offset-sided	29.95	____
(260)	SLSF 2-bay Hopper, offset-sided	29.95	____
(261)	LNE 2-bay Hopper, offset-sided	29.95	____
(262)	D&H 2-bay Hopper, offset-sided	29.95	____
(263)	NKP 2-bay Hopper, offset-sided	29.95	____
(264)	MP 2-bay Hopper, offset-sided	29.95	____
(265)	Conrail 2-bay Hopper, offset-sided	29.95	____
(266)	CNW 2-bay Hopper, offset-sided	29.95	____
(267)	Monon 2-bay Hopper, offset-sided	29.95	____
(268)	B&O 2-bay Hopper, offset-sided	29.95	____
(352)	CP 2-bay Hopper, offset-sided	29.95	____
(355)	IC 2-bay Hopper, offset-sided	29.95	____
(359)	IIP 2-bay Hopper, offset-sided	29.95	____
(361)	LNE 2-bay Hopper, offset-sided	29.95	____
(364)	MP 2-bay Hopper, offset-sided	29.95	____
(366)	CNW 2-bay Hopper, offset-sided	29.95	____
(368)	B&O 2-bay Hopper, offset-sided	29.95	____
(420)	BN Gondola	29.95	____
(500)	Undecorated Tank Car	36.95	____
(501)	CPC INT Tank Car	36.95	____
(502)	GATX Tank Car	36.95	____
(503)	Cargill Tank Car	36.95	____
(504)	JM Huber Tank Car	36.95	____
(505)	Englehard Tank Car	36.95	____
(506)	Georgia Kao Tank Car	36.95	____
(507)	N.J. Zinc Tank Car	36.95	____
(508)	BASF Wyand Tank Car	36.95	____

		Retail	Cond/$
(509)	American Maize Tank Car	36.95	____
(510)	B.F. Goodrich Tank Car	36.95	____
(511)	Elcor Chemical Tank Car	36.95	____
(512)	Domino Sugar Tank Car	36.95	____
(772)	Automatic Water Tower	79.95	____
(774)	Floodlight Tower	79.95	____
(1100)	Undecorated 40' Boxcar	30.95	____
(1100)	WFE 40' Boxcar Premium series	31.95	____
(1102)	B&O 40' Boxcar	30.95	____
(1103)	SSW/SP 40' Boxcar	30.95	____
(1105)	D&RGW 40' Boxcar	30.95	____
(1105)	BN/WFE 40' Boxcar "76120"	32.95	____
(1108)	GN 40' Boxcar, Classic series	34.95	____
(1112)	Soo Line 40' Boxcar	24.95	____
(1113)	NYC 40' Boxcar	30.95	____
(1114)	PRR 40' Boxcar	30.95	____
(1115)	ATSF 40' Boxcar	30.95	____
(1116)	SEA 40' Boxcar	30.95	____
(1117)	SP 40' Boxcar	30.95	____
(1118)	UP 40' Boxcar	30.95	____
(1119)	C&O 40' Boxcar	30.95	____
(1121)	NYC 40' Boxcar, Classic series	34.95	____
(1122)	RUT 40' Boxcar, Classic series	34.95	____
(1125)	P&LE 40' Boxcar, Premium series	31.95	____
(1126)	NP40' Boxcar, Premium series	31.95	____
(1128)	NH 40' Boxcar	30.95	____
(1129)	GN 40' Boxcar	30.95	____
(1130)	GM&O 40' Boxcar	30.95	____
(1131)	N&W 40' Boxcar	30.95	____
(1132)	CP 40' Boxcar	30.95	____
(1133)	M&StL 40' Boxcar	30.95	____
(1133)	NYC 40' Boxcar "180454"	30.95	____
(1134)	Erie Lackawanna 40' Boxcar	30.95	____
(1135)	SP 40'' Boxcar, Premium series	31.95	____
(1136)	Susie-Q 40' Boxcar, Classic series	34.95	____
(1137)	CNW 40' Boxcar	30.95	____
(1138)	CR 40' Boxcar	30.95	____
(1500)	Undecorated 50' Ribbed Boxcar	36.95	____
(1501)	Railbox 50' Ribbed Boxcar	36.95	____
(1502)	Evergreen 50' Ribbed Boxcar	36.95	____
(1503)	MEC 50' Ribbed Boxcar	36.95	____
(1504)	CNW 50' Ribbed Boxcar	36.95	____
(1505)	UP 50' Ribbed Boxcar	39.95	____
(1506)	Conrail 50' Ribbed Boxcar	36.95	____
(1507)	BN 50' Ribbed Boxcar	36.95	____
(1508)	Tropicana 50' Ribbed Boxcar	36.95	____
(1509)	D&RGW 50' Ribbed Boxcar	36.95	____
(1510)	Rail Link 50' Ribbed Boxcar	36.95	____

		Retail	Cond/S
(1511)	CSX Link 50' Ribbed Boxcar	36.95	____
(1512)	Soo 50' Ribbed Boxcar	36.95	____
(1513)	Miller 50' Ribbed Boxcar	36.95	____
(1514)	PRR 50' Ribbed Boxcar	36.95	____
(1515)	NYC 50' Ribbed Boxcar	36.95	____
(1516)	Amtrak 50' Ribbed Boxcar	36.95	____
(2200)	Undecorated 40' Plug Door Boxcar	30.95	____
(2202)	PFE 40' Boxcar, Premium series	32.95	____
(2203)	ART 40' Boxcar, Premium series	32.95	____
(2204)	PGE 40' Boxcar, Premium series	32.95	____
(2206)	Dubuque 40' Boxcar, Premium series	32.95	____
(2207)	WP 40' Plug Door Boxcar	30.95	____
(2208)	CN 40' Plug Door Boxcar	30.95	____
(2209)	DT&I 40' Boxcar, Premium series	34.95	____
(2210)	ATSF 40' Boxcar, Premium series	34.95	____
(2211)	PRR 40' Plug Door Boxcar	30.95	____
(2212)	Soo Line 40' Plug Door Boxcar	30.95	____
(2213)	MILW 40' Plug Door Boxcar	30.95	____
(2215)	NYC 40' Boxcar, Premium series	34.95	____
(2216)	BN 40' Boxcar, Premium series	34.95	____
(2217)	GN 40' Plug Door Boxcar	30.95	____
(2218)	CP 40' Plug Door Boxcar	30.95	____
(2219)	PG&E 40' Plug Door Boxcar	30.95	____
(2220)	B&A 40' Boxcar Classic series	33.95	____
(2221)	NP 40' Boxcar Classic series	33.95	____
(2222)	Miller 40' Plug Door Boxcar	30.95	____
(2223)	BNE Classic 40' Plug Door Boxcar	33.95	____
(2224)	CP Classic 40' Plug Door Boxcar	33.95	____
(2225)	Frisco Classic 40' Plug Door Boxcar	33.95	____
(2226)	ADM 40' Plug Door Boxcar	39.95	____
(3200)	Undecorated 2-bay Hopper, rib-sided	30.95	____
(3201)	C&O 2-bay Hopper, rib-sided	30.95	____
(3202)	WM 2-bay Hopper, rib-sided	30.05	____
(3203)	D&O 2-bay Hopper, rib-sided	30.95	____
(3204)	Erie 2-bay Hopper, rib-sided	30.95	____
(3205)	N&W 2-bay Hopper, rib-sided	30.95	____
(3206)	NYC 2-bay Hopper, rib-sided	30.95	____
(3206R)	NYC red 2-bay Hopper, rib-sided	30.95	____
(3207)	PRR 2-bay Hopper, rib-sided	30.95	____
(3208)	Peabody 2-bay Hopper, rib-sided	30.95	____
(3209)	Southern 2-bay Hopper, rib-sided	30.95	____
(3211)	SP 2-bay Hopper, rib-sided	30.95	____
(3213)	Virginia 2-bay Hopper, rib-sided	30.95	____
(3214)	RDG 2-bay Hopper, rib-sided	30.95	____
(3215)	CB&Q 2-bay Hopper, rib-sided	30.95	____
(3216)	LV 2-bay Hopper, rib-sided	30.95	____
(3217)	Interstate RR 2-bay Hopper, rib-sided	30.95	____
(3218)	Burlington 2-bay Hopper, rib-sided	30.95	____

		Retail	Cond/$
(3218)	D&RGW 2-bay Hopper, rib-sided	30.95	____
(3219)	NH 2-bay Hopper, rib-sided	30.95	____
(3251)	ATSF 2-bay Hopper, offset-sided	30.95	____
(3252)	CP 2-bay Hopper, offset-sided	30.95	____
(3253)	GN 2-bay Hopper, offset-sided	30.95	____
(3254)	NP 2-bay Hopper, offset-sided	30.95	____
(3255)	IC 2-bay Hopper, offset-sided	30.95	____
(3256)	NYC 2-bay Hopper, offset-sided	30.95	____
(3257)	L&N 2-bay Hopper, offset-sided	30.95	____
(3258)	Milwaukee 2-bay Hopper, offset-sided	30.95	____
(3259)	UP 2-bay Hopper, offset-sided	30.95	____
(3260)	Frisco 2-bay Hopper, offset-sided	30.95	____
(3261)	LNE 2-bay Hopper, offset-sided	30.95	____
(3262)	D&H 2-bay Hopper, offset-sided	30.95	____
(3263)	NKP 2-bay Hopper, offset-sided	30.95	____
(3264)	MP 2-bay Hopper, offset-sided	30.95	____
(3265)	Conrail 2-bay Hopper, offset-sided	30.95	____
(3266)	C&NW 2-bay Hopper, offset-sided	30.95	____
(3267)	Monon 2-bay Hopper, offset-sided	30.95	____
(3268)	B&O 2-bay Hopper, offset-sided	30.95	____
(3269)	ACL 2-bay Hopper, offset-sided	30.95	____
(3270)	GM&O 2-bay Hopper, offset-sided	30.95	____
(3271)	RDG 2-bay Hopper, offset-sided	30.95	____
(3272)	Rock Island 2-bay Hopper, offset-sided	30.95	____
(3272)	Southern 2-bay Hopper, offset-sided	30.95	____
(3273)	RDG Blue Coal 2-bay Hopper, offset-sided	30.95	____
(3300)	Undecorated PS-2 CD 3-bay Hopper	39.95	____
(3301)	A.D.M. PS-2 CD 3-bay Hopper "2114"	39.95	____
(3302)	BN PS-2 CD 3-bay Hopper "450995"	39.95	____
(3303)	Cargill PS-2 CD 3-bay Hopper "TLDX 2520"	39.95	____
(3304)	C&NW PS-2 CD 3-bay Hopper "96758"	39.95	____
(3305)	Conrail PS-2 CD 3-bay Hopper "865781"	39.95	____
(3306)	GN PS-2 CD 3-bay Hopper "172213"	39.95	____
(3307)	IC PS-2 CD 3-bay Hopper "54607"	39.95	____
(3308)	PRR PS-2 CD 3-bay Hopper "260084"	39.95	____
(3309)	Pillsbury PS-2 CD 3-bay Hopper "3089"	39.95	____
(3310)	D&RGW PS-2 CD 3-bay Hopper "15045"	39.95	____
(3311)	The Rock PS-2 CD 3-bay Hopper "13278"	39.95	____
(3312)	AT&SF PS-2 CD 3-bay Hopper "304227"	39.95	____
(3313)	UP PS-2 CD 3-bay Hopper "21753"	39.95	____
(3400)	Undecorated 4-bay Hopper	33.95	____
(3401)	B&O 4-bay Hopper "532161"	33.95	____
(3402)	C&O 4-bay Hopper "67297"	33.95	____
(3403)	IC 4-bay Hopper "67049"	33.95	____
(3404)	NH 4-bay Hopper "81225"	33.95	____
(3405)	MP 4-bay Hopper "1912"	33.95	____
(3406)	Peabody Coal 4-bay Hopper "8676"	33.95	____
(3407)	Rock Island 4-bay Hopper "133288"	33.95	____

		Retail	Cond/$
(3408)	AT&SF 4-bay Hopper "181040"	33.95	____
(3409)	WM 4-bay Hopper "15308"	33.95	____
(3410)	NYC 4-bay Hopper "904641"	33.95	____
(3411)	NP 4-bay Hopper	33.95	____
(3414)	RDG Blue Coal 4-bay Hopper	33.95	____
(3451)	BN 4-bay Hopper "514024"	33.95	____
(3452)	CB&Q 4-bay Hopper "171426"	33.95	____
(3453)	C&NW 4-bay Hopper "64651"	33.95	____
(3454)	CR 4-bay Hopper "403122"	33.95	____
(3455)	CSX 4-bay Hopper "311566"	33.95	____
(3456)	D&RGW 4-bay Hopper "12543"	33.95	____
(3457)	GN 4-bay Hopper "705014"	33.95	____
(3458R)	PRR 4-bay Hopper "923678"	33.95	____
(3458B)	GN 4-bay Hopper "918295"	33.95	____
(3459)	UP 4-bay Hopper "901423"	33.95	____
(3460)	SP 4-bay Hopper "43277"	33.95	____
(3461)	Virginian 4-bay Hopper "9059"	33.95	____
(4400)	Undecorated Gondola	30.95	____
(4401)	SLSF Gondola	30.95	____
(4401)	Frisco Gondola "61760"	30.95	____
(4402)	Wabash Gondola	30.95	____
(4402)	BN Gondola "565557"	30.95	____
(4403)	Southern Gondola	30.95	____
(4404)	PRR Gondola	30.95	____
(4405)	GN Gondola	30.95	____
(4406)	LV Gondola	30.95	____
(4407)	B&O Gondola	30.95	____
(4408)	C&O Gondola	30.95	____
(4409)	MILW Gondola	30.95	____
(4410)	SP Gondola	30.95	____
(4411)	WM Gondola	30.95	____
(4412)	Soo Line Gondola	30.95	____
(4413)	Lackawanna Gondola	30.95	____
(4414)	IC Gondola	30.95	____
(4415)	NYC Gondola	30.95	____
(4416)	NKP Gondola	30.95	____
(4417)	N&W Gondola	30.95	____
(4418)	UP Gondola	30.95	____
(4419)	ATSF Gondola	30.95	____
(4420)	BN Gondola	30.95	____
(4421)	CP Gondola	30.95	____
(4422)	NP Gondola	30.95	____
(4423)	D&H Gondola	30.95	____
(4424)	Reading Gondola	30.95	____
(4425)	D&RGW Gondola	30.95	____
(4426)	CNW Gondola	30.95	____
(4427)	CR Gondola	30.95	____
(4428)	MP Gondola	30.95	____

		Retail	Cond/$
(4429)	CB&Q Gondola	31.95	____
(4430)	NH Gondola	31.95	____
(4431)	P&LE Gondola	31.95	____
(4432)	RI Gondola	31.95	____
(6000)	Undecorated USRA 46' Flatcar	37.95	____
(6001)	B&O USRA 46' Flatcar	37.95	____
(6002)	Burlington Route USRA 46' Flatcar	37.95	____
(6003)	BN USRA 46' Flatcar	37.95	____
(6004)	Conrail USRA 46' Flatcar	37.95	____
(6005)	C&NW USRA 46' Flatcar	37.95	____
(6006)	C&O USRA 46' Flatcar	37.95	____
(6007)	CSX USRA 46' Flatcar	37.95	____
(6008)	CP USRA 46' Flatcar	37.95	____
(6009)	D&RGW USRA 46' Flatcar	37.95	____
(6010)	GN USRA 46' Flatcar	37.95	____
(6011)	IC USRA 46' Flatcar	37.95	____
(6012)	NH USRA 46' Flatcar	37.95	____
(6013)	NYC USRA 46' Flatcar	37.95	____
(6014)	NP USRA 46' Flatcar	37.95	____
(6015)	N&W USRA 46' Flatcar	37.95	____
(6016)	MP USRA 46' Flatcar	37.95	____
(6017)	PRR USRA 46' Flatcar	37.95	____
(6018)	ATSF USRA 46' Flatcar	37.95	____
(6019)	Southern USRA 46' Flatcar	37.95	____
(6020)	SP USRA 46' Flatcar	37.95	____
(6021)	UP USRA 46' Flatcar	37.95	____
(6022)	Frisco USRA 46' Flatcar	37.95	____
(6024)	RI USRA 46' Flatcar	37.95	____
(7501)	ATSF Wood-sided Caboose	39.95	____
(7502)	ACL Wood-sided Caboose	39.95	____
(7503)	B&O Wood-sided Caboose	39.95	____
(7504)	CP Wood-sided Caboose	39.95	____
(7505)	CB&Q Wood-sided Caboose	39.95	____
(7506)	C&O Wood-sided Caboose	39.95	____
(7507)	C&NW Wood-sided Caboose	39.95	____
(7508)	D&RG Wood-sided Caboose	39.95	____
(7509)	Erie Wood-sided Caboose	39.95	____
(7510)	Frisco Wood-sided Caboose	39.95	____
(7511)	GN Wood-sided Caboose	39.95	____
(7512)	GM&O Wood-sided Caboose	39.95	____
(7513)	IC Wood-sided Caboose	39.95	____
(7514)	Lackawanna Wood-sided Caboose	39.95	____
(7515)	Milwaukee Road Wood-sided Caboose	39.95	____
(7516)	MP Wood-sided Caboose	39.95	____
(7517)	NH Wood-sided Caboose	39.95	____
(7518)	NYC Wood-sided Caboose	39.95	____
(7519)	N&W Wood-sided Caboose	39.95	____
(7520)	NP Wood-sided Caboose	39.95	____

		Retail	Cond/$
(7521)	PRR Wood-sided Caboose	39.95	____
(7522)	RI Wood-sided Caboose	39.95	____
(7523)	Southern Wood-sided Caboose	39.95	____
(7524)	SP Wood-sided Caboose	39.95	____
(7525)	UP Wood-sided Caboose	39.95	____
(7526)	Rio Grande 4-stripe Wood-sided Caboose	39.95	____
(7527)	NYC Pacemaker Wood-sided Caboose	39.95	____
(7700)	Undecorated Caboose	36.95	____
(7701)	Chessie Caboose	36.95	____
(7702)	Erie Caboose	36.95	____
(7703)	Erie Lackawanna Caboose, red	36.95	____
(7704)	Conrail Caboose	36.95	____
(7705)	CNW Caboose	36.95	____
(7705)	Southern Caboose	36.95	____
(7707)	NYC Caboose	36.95	____
(7708)	PRR Caboose	36.95	____
(7709)	NW Caboose	36.95	____
(7710)	ATSF Caboose	36.95	____
(7711)	SP Caboose	36.95	____
(7712)	GN Caboose	36.95	____
(7713)	NP Caboose	36.95	____
(7714)	UP Caboose	36.95	____
(7715)	NH Caboose	36.95	____
(7716)	CP Caboose	36.95	____
(7718)	Erie-Lackawanna Caboose, maroon and gray	38.95	____
(7719)	BN Caboose	36.95	____
(7720)	Burlington Caboose "1113"	38.95	____
(7721)	Milwaukee Road B/W Caboose	39.95	____
(7722)	SLSF B/W premium Caboose	41.95	____
(7723)	MP B/W Caboose	39.95	____
(7724)	CSX B/W Caboose	39.95	____
(7725)	NYC B/W Caboose	39.95	____
(7726)	SP B/W Caboose	39.95	____
(46000)	Undecorated USRA 4-0-2	349.95	____
(46000AC)	Undecorated USRA 4-6-2 Pacific Steam Locomotive	379.95	____
(46000AC-GN)	Great Northern USRA 4-6-2 Pacific Steam Locomotive	379.95	____
(46000AC-NP)	Northern Pacific USRA 4-6-2 Pacific Steam Locomotive	379.95	____
(46000AC-NYC)	NYC USRA 4-6-2 Pacific Steam Locomotive	379.95	____
(46000AC-PRR)	PRR USRA 4-6-2 Pacific Steam Locomotive	379.95	____
(46000AC-SF)	Santa Fe USRA 4-6-2 Pacific Steam Locomotive	379.95	____
(46000AC-WO)	Undecorated USRA 4-6-2 Pacific Steam Locomotive w/ Limited Sounds	329.95	____

	Retail	Cond/$
(46000AC-WO-GN) Great Northern USRA 4-6-2 Pacific Steam Locomotive w/ Limited Sounds	329.95	____
(46000AC-WO-NP) Northern Pacific USRA 4-6-2 Pacific Steam Locomotive w/ Limited Sounds	329.95	____
(46000AC-WO-NYC) NYC USRA 4-6-2 Pacific Steam Locomotive w/ Limited Sounds	329.95	____
(46000AC-WO-PRR) PRR USRA 4-6-2 Pacific Steam Locomotive w/ Limited Sounds	329.95	____
(46000AC-WO-SF) Santa Fe USRA 4-6-2 Pacific Steam Locomotive w/ Limited Sounds	329.95	____
(46000HR) Undecorated USRA 4-6-2 Pacific Steam Locomotive (Hi-Rail Version)	299.95	____
(46000HR-GN) Great Northern USRA 4-6-2 Pacific Steam Locomotive (Hi-Rail Version)	299.95	____
(46000HR-NP) Northern Pacific USRA 4-6-2 Pacific Steam Locomotive (Hi-Rail Version)	299.95	____
(46000HR-NYC) NYC USRA 4-6-2 Pacific Steam Locomotive (Hi-Rail Version)	299.95	____
(46000HR-PRR) PRR USRA 4-6-2 Pacific Steam Locomotive (Hi-Rail Version)	299.95	____
(46000HR-SF) Santa Fe USRA 4-6-2 Pacific Steam Locomotive (Hi-Rail Version)	299.95	____
(46000S) Undecorated USRA 4-6-2 Pacific Steam Locomotive (DC Scale Version)	299.95	____
(46000S-GN) Great Northern USRA 4-6-2 Pacific Steam Locomotive (DC Scale Version)	299.95	____
(46000S-NP) Northern Pacific USRA 4-6-2 Pacific Steam Locomotive (DC Scale Version)	299.95	____
(46000S-NYC) NYC USRA 4-6-2 Pacific Steam Locomotive (DC Scale Version)	299.95	____
(46000S-PRR) PRR USRA 4-6-2 Pacific Steam Locomotive (DC Scale Version)	299.95	____
(46000S-SF) Santa Fe USRA 4-6-2 Pacific Steam Locomotive (DC Scale Version)	299.95	____
(46001) B&O USRA 4-6-2	349.95	____
(46002AC) Southern USRA 4-6-2 Pacific Steam Locomotive	379.95	____
(46002AC-WO) Southern USRA 4-6-2 Pacific Steam Locomotive w/ Limited Sounds	329.95	____
(46002HR) Southern USRA 4-6-2 Pacific Steam Locomotive (Hi-Rail Version)	299.95	____
(46002S) Southern USRA 4-6-2 Pacific Steam Locomotive (DC Scale Version)	299.95	____
(46002) Southern USRA 4-6-2	349.95	____
(46003AC) Milwaukee Road USRA 4-6-2 Pacific Steam Locomotive	379.95	____
(46003AC-WO) Milwaukee Road USRA 4-6-2 Pacific Locomotive w/ Limited Sounds	329.95	____

	Retail	Cond/$
(46003HR) Milwaukee Road USRA 4-6-2 Pacific Locomotive (Hi-Rail Version)	299.95	___
(46003S) Milwaukee Road USRA 4-6-2 Pacific Steam Locomotive (DC Scale Version)	299.95	___
(46004AC) New Haven USRA 4-6-2 Pacific Steam Locomotive	379.95	___
(46004AC-WO) New Haven USRA 4-6-2 Pacific Steam Locomotive w/ Limited Sounds	329.95	___
(46004HR) New Haven USRA 4-6-2 Pacific Steam Locomotive (Hi-Rail Version)	299.95	___
(46004S) New Haven USRA 4-6-2 Pacific Steam Locomotive (DC Scale Version)	299.95	___
(46500) Undecorated USRA 4-6-2	619.95	___
(46500AC) Undecorated USRA 4-6-2 Pacific Steam Passenger set	699.95	___
(46500HR) Undecorated USRA 4-6-2 Pacific Steam Passenger set (Hi-Rail)	619.95	___
(46500S) Undecorated USRA 4-6-2 Pacific Steam Passenger set (DC Scale)	619.95	___
(46501) B&O USRA 4-6-2	619.95	___
(46502) Southern USRA 4-6-2	619.95	___
(46502AC) Southern USRA 4-6-2 Pacific Steam Passenger set	699.95	___
(46502HR) Southern USRA 4-6-2 Pacific Steam Passenger set (Hi-Rail)	619.95	___
(46502S) Southern USRA 4-6-2 Pacific Steam Passenger set (DC Scale)	619.95	___
(46503AC) Milwaukee Road USRA 4-6-2 Pacific Steam Passenger set	659.95	___
(46503HR) Milwaukee Road USRA 4-6-2 Pacific Steam Passenger set (Hi-Rail)	599.95	___
(46503S) Milwaukee Road USRA 4-6-2 Pacific Steam Passenger set (DC Scale)	599.95	___
(46504AC) New Haven USRA 4-6-2 Pacific Steam Passenger set	699.95	___
(46504HR) New Haven USRA 4-6-2 Pacific Steam Passenger set (Hi-Rail)	619.95	___
(46504S) New Haven USRA 4-6-2 Pacific Steam Passenger set (DC Scale)	619.95	___
(BD8201) B&O Budd Coach	74.95	___
(BD8202) Southern Budd Coach	74.95	___
(BD8203) UP Budd Coach	74.95	___
(BD8205) NYC Budd Coach	84.95	___
(BD8206) ATSF Budd Coach	74.95	___
(BD8209) PRR Budd Coach	74.95	___
(BD8214) ACL Budd Coach	74.95	___
(BD8215) Burlington Budd Coach	74.95	___
(BD8216) RI Budd Coach	74.95	___

	Retail	Cond/S
(BD8218) Central of Georgia Budd Coach	74.95	____
(BDB8217) IC Budd Coach	74.95	____
(BDBS00) Undecorated, silver Budd Coach	74.95	____
(BDBS00) Undecorated, silver Budd 4-car set	289.95	____
(BDBS01) B&O Budd 4-car set	319.95	____
(BDBS02) Southern Budd 4-car set	319.95	____
(BDBS03) UP Budd 4-car set	319.95	____
(BDBS05) NYC 4-car Budd set	319.95	____
(BDBS06) ATSF Budd 4-car set	319.95	____
(BDBS09) PRR Budd 4-car set	319.95	____
(BDBS14) ACL Budd 4-car set	319.95	____
(BDBS15) Burlington Budd 4-car set	319.95	____
(BDBS16) RI Budd 4-car set	319.95	____
(BDBS17) IC Budd 4-car set	319.95	____
(BDBS18) Central of Georgia Budd 4-car set	319.95	____
(BSSC1) Conrail Trailer Hauler Freight set	299.95	____
(BSSC4) SP Trailer Hauler Freight set	299.95	____
(CB208S) Ground Throw	2.70	____
(DXF211AB) B&O FA AB w/ sound	489.95	____
(DXF211ABA) B&O FA ABA w/ sound	359.95	____
(DXF211ABPW) B&O FA AB powered B	359.95	____
(DXF214AB) Rock Island FA AB w/ sound	489.95	____
(DXF214ABA) Rock Island FA ABA w/ sound	359.95	____
(DXF214ABPW) Rock Island FA AB powered B	359.95	____
(DXF710AB) Atlantic Coast Line FP7 AB w/ sound	359.95	____
(DXF710ABA) ACL FP7 AB w/ sound	489.95	____
(DXF710ABPW) ACL FP7 AB w/ powered B	359.95	____
(DXF711AB) B&O FP7 AB w/ sound	359.95	____
(DXF711ABA) B&O FP7 ABA w/ sound	489.95	____
(DXF711ABPW) B&O FP7 AB w/ powered B	359.95	____
(DXF712AB) C&O FP7 AB w/ sound	359.95	____
(DXF712ABA) C&O FP7 ABA w/ sound	489.95	____
(DXF712ABPW) C&O FP7 AB w/ powered B	359.95	____
(DXF713AB) D&RG FP7 AB w/ sound	359.95	____
(DXF713ABA) D&RG FP7 ABA w/ sound	489.95	____
(DXF713ABPW) D&RG FP7 AB w/ powered B	359.95	____
(DXF714AB) Rock Island FP7 AB w/ sound	359.95	____
(DXF714ABA) Rock Island FP7 ABA w/ sound	489.95	____
(DXF714ABPW) Rock Island FP7 AB w/ powered B	359.95	____
(DXF715AB) Southern FP7 AB w/ powered B	359.95	____
(DXF715AB) Southern FP7 AB w/ sound	489.95	____
(DXF715ABA) Southern FP7 ABA w/ sound	359.95	____
(DXFA2011) B&O FA A Unit	199.95	____
(DXFA2014) Rock Island FA A Unit	199.95	____
(DXFA211DNS) B&O FA B Unit w/ sound	199.95	____
(DXFB211PW) B&O FA B Unit powered	199.95	____
(DXFB214PW) Rock Island B Unit powered	199.95	____
(DXFB214SND) Rock Island B Unit w/ sound	199.95	____

		Retail	Cond/$
(DXFB710PW) ACL FP7 B Unit powered		199.95	___
(DXFB711PW) B&O FP7 B Unit powered		199.95	___
(DXFB711SND) B&O FP7 B Unit w/ sound		199.95	___
(DXFB712PW) C&O FP7 B Unit powered		199.95	___
(DXFB712SND) C&O FP7 B Unit w/ sound		199.95	___
(DXFB713PW) D&RG FP7 B Unit powered		199.95	___
(DXFB713SND) D&RG FP7 B Unit w/ sound		199.95	___
(DXFB714) Rock Island FP7 A Unit		199.95	___
(DXFB714PW) Rock Island FP7 B unit powered		199.95	___
(DXFB714SND) Rock Island FP7 B Unit w/ sound		199.95	___
(DXFB715PW) Southern FP7 B Unit powered		199.95	___
(DXFB715SND) Southern FP7 B Unit w/ sound		199.95	___
(DXFP7010) ACL FP7 A Unit		199.95	___
(DXFP7011) B&O FP7 A Unit		199.95	___
(DXFP7012) C&O FP7 A Unit		199.95	___
(DXFP7013) D&RG FP7 A Unit		199.95	___
(DXFP715) Southern FP7 A Unit		199.95	___
(DXFP7B710SND) ACL FP7 B Unit w/ sound		199.95	___
(E800) Undecorated E8 Diesel		299.95	___
(E800AA) Undecorated E8 Diesel AA		549.95	___
(E803) NYC E8 Diesel		299.95	___
(E803AA) NYC E8 Diesel AA		549.95	___
(E805) PRR E8 Diesel		299.95	___
(E805AA) PRR E8 Diesel AA (Tuscan red)		549.95	___
(E806) PRR E8 Diesel (Brunswick green)		299.95	___
(E806AA) PRR E8 Diesel AA (Brunswick green)		549.95	___
(E808) UP E8 Diesel		299.95	___
(E808AA) UP E8 Diesel AA		549.95	___
(E811) B&O E8 Diesel		299.95	___
(E811AA) B&O E8 Diesel AA		549.95	___
(E816) ATSF E8 Diesel		299.95	___
(E817) Burlington E8 Diesel		299.95	___
(E818) Central of Georgia E8 Diesel		299.95	___
(E819) Burlington E8 Diesel		299.95	___
(E819AA) Burlington E8 Diesel AA		549.95	___
(E820) IC E8 Diesel		299.95	___
(E820AA) IC E8 Diesel AA		549.95	___
(E821) Central of Georgia E8 Diesel		299.95	___
(E821AA) Central of Georgia E8 Diesel AA		549.95	___
(ESE01) Empire State Express set		699.95	___
(F40P2) Amtrak EMD F-40 PH-2		199.95	___
(F40P3) Amtrak EMD F-40 PH-3		199.95	___
(F200AB) Undecorated FA-2 Diesel AB w/ sound		349.95	___
(F200ABA) Undecorated FA-2 Diesel ABA w/ sound		479.95	___
(F200ABPW) Undecorated FA-2 Diesel AB powered		349.95	___
(F201AB) CP FA-2 Diesel AB w/ sound		349.95	___
(F201ABA) CP FA-2 Diesel ABA w/ sound		479.95	___
(F201ABPW) CP FA-2 Diesel AB powered		349.95	___

	Retail	Cond/S
(F202AB) GN FA-2 Diesel AB w/ sound	349.95	____
(F202ABA) GN FA-2 Diesel ABA w/ sound	479.95	____
(F202ABPW) GN FA-2 Diesel AB powered	349.95	____
(F203AB) NH FA-2 Diesel AB w/ sound	349.95	____
(F203ABA) NH FA-2 Diesel ABA w/ sound	479.95	____
(F203ABPW) NH FA-2 Diesel AB powered	349.95	____
(F204AB) NYC FA-2 Diesel AB w/ sound	349.95	____
(F204ABA) NYC FA-2 Diesel ABA w/ sound	479.95	____
(F204ABPW) NYC FA-2 Diesel AB powered	349.95	____
(F205AB) UP FA-2 Diesel AB w/ sound	349.95	____
(F205ABA) UP FA-2 Diesel ABA w/ sound	479.95	____
(F205ABPW) UP FA-2 Diesel AB powered	349.95	____
(F206AB) PRR FA-2 Diesel AB w/ sound	349.95	____
(F206ABA) PRR FA-2 Diesel ABA w/ sound	479.95	____
(F206ABPW) PRR FA-2 Diesel AB powered	349.95	____
(F700AB) Undecorated FP-7 Diesel AB w/ sound	349.95	____
(F700ABA) Undecorated FP-7 Diesel ABA w/ sound	479.95	____
(F700ABPW) Undecorated FP-7 Diesel AB powered	349.95	____
(F701AB) BN FP-7 Diesel AB w/ sound	349.95	____
(F701ABA) BN FP-7 Diesel ABA w/ sound	479.95	____
(F701ABPW) BN FP-7 Diesel AB powered	349.95	____
(F702AB) GN FP-7 Diesel AB w/ sound	349.95	____
(F702ABA) GN FP-7 Diesel ABA w/ sound	479.95	____
(F702ABPW) GN FP-7 Diesel AB powered	349.95	____
(F703AB) NYC FP-7 Diesel AB w/ sound	349.95	____
(F703ABA) NYC FP-7 Diesel ABA, gray, w/ sound	479.95	____
(F703ABPW) NYC FP-7 Diesel AB, gray, powered	349.95	____
(F704AB) NP FP-7 Diesel AB w/ sound	349.95	____
(F704ABA) NP FP-7 Diesel ABA w/ sound	479.95	____
(F704ABPW) NP FP-7 Diesel AB powered	349.95	____
(F705AB) PRR FP-7 Diesel AB w/ sound	349.95	____
(F705ABA) PRR FP-7 Diesel ABA, red, w/ sound	479.95	____
(F705ABPW) PRR FP-7 Diesel AB, red, powered	349.95	____
(F706AB) PRR FP-7 Diesel AB w/ sound	349.95	____
(F706ABA) PRR FP-7 Diesel ABA, green, w/ sound	479.95	____
(F706ABPW) PRR FP-7 Diesel AB, green, powered	349.95	____
(F707AB) SP FP-7 Diesel AB w/ sound	349.95	____
(F707ABA) SP FP-7 Diesel ABA w/ sound	479.95	____
(F707ABPW) SP FP-7 Diesel AB powered	349.95	____
(F708AB) UP FP-7 Diesel AB w/ sound	349.95	____
(F708ABA) UP FP-7 Diesel ABA w/ sound	479.95	____
(F708ABPW) UP FP-7 Diesel AB powered	349.95	____
(F709AB) NYC FP-7 Diesel AB w/ sound	349.95	____
(F709ABA) NYC FP-7 Diesel ABA, black, w/ sound	479.95	____
(F7B00PW) Undecorated FP-7 Diesel B Unit powered	189.95	____
(F709ABPW) NYC FP-7 Diesel AB, black, powered	349.95	____
(F7B00SND) Undecorated FP-7 Diesel B Unit w/ sound	189.95	____
(F7B01PW) BN FP-7 Diesel B Unit powered	189.95	____

	Retail	Cond/$
(F7B01SND) BN FP-7 Diesel B Unit w/ sound	189.95	____
(F7B02PW) GN FP-7 Diesel B Unit powered	189.95	____
(F7B02SND) GN FP-7 Diesel B Unit w/ sound	189.95	____
(F7B03PW) NYC FP-7 Diesel B Unit, gray, powered	189.95	____
(F7B03SND) NYC FP-7 Diesel B Unit, gray, w/ sound	189.95	____
(F7B04PW) NP FP-7 Diesel B Unit powered	189.95	____
(F7B04SND) NP FP-7 Diesel B Unit w/ sound	189.95	____
(F7B05PW) PRR FP-7 Diesel B Unit, red, powered	189.95	____
(F7B05SND) PRR FP-7 Diesel B Unit, red, w/ sound	189.95	____
(F7B06PW) PRR FP-7 Diesel B Unit, green, powered	189.95	____
(F7B06SND) PRR FP-7 Diesel B Unit, green, w/ sound	189.95	____
(F7B07PW) SP FP-7 Diesel B Unit powered	189.95	____
(F7B07SND) SP FP-7 Diesel B Unit w/ sound	189.95	____
(F7B08PW) UP FP-7 Diesel B Unit powered	189.95	____
(F7B08SND) UP FP-7 Diesel B Unit w/ sound	189.95	____
(F7B09PW) NYC FP-7 Diesel B Unit, black, powered	189.95	____
(F7B09SND) NYC FP-7 Diesel B Unit, black, w/ sound	189.95	____
(FA2000) Undecorated Alco FA-2	189.95	____
(FA2001) CP Alco FA-2	189.95	____
(FA2002) GN Alco FA-2	189.95	____
(FA2003) NH Alco FA-2 "10401"	189.95	____
(FA2004) NYC Alco FA-2	189.95	____
(FA2005) UP Alco FA-2	189.95	____
(FA2006) PRR Alco FB-2	189.95	____
(FB2000) Undecorated Alco FB-2	189.95	____
(FB2001) CP Alco FB-2	189.95	____
(FB2002) GN Alco FB-2	189.95	____
(FB2003) NH Alco FB-2	189.95	____
(FB2004) NYC Alco FB-2	189.95	____
(FB2005) UP Alco FB-2	189.95	____
(FB2006) PRR Alco FB-2	189.95	____
(FB200PW) Undecorated FA-2 Diesel B Unit powered	189.95	____
(FB200SND) Undecorated FA-2 Diesel B Unit w/ sound	189.95	____
(FB201PW) CP FA-2 Diesel B Unit powered	189.95	____
(FB201SND) CP FA-2 Diesel B Unit w/ sound	189.95	____
(FB202PW) GN FA-2 Diesel B Unit powered	189.95	____
(FB202SND) GN FA-2 Diesel B Unit w/ sound	189.95	____
(FB203PW) NH FA-2 Diesel B Unit powered	189.95	____
(FB203SND) NH FA-2 Diesel B Unit w/ sound	189.95	____
(FB204PW) NYC FA-2 Diesel B Unit powered	189.95	____
(FB204SND) NYC FA-2 Diesel B Unit w/ sound	189.95	____
(FB205PW) UP FA-2 Diesel B Unit powered	189.95	____
(FB205SND) UP FA-2 Diesel B Unit w/ sound	189.95	____
(FB206PW) PRR FA-2 Diesel B Unit powered	189.95	____
(FB206SND) PRR FA-2 Diesel B Unit w/ sound	189.95	____
(FB7000) Undecorated EMD FB-7	189.95	____
(FB7001) BN EMD FB-7	189.95	____

		Retail	Cond/S
(FB7002)	GN EMD FB-7	189.95	____
(FB7003)	NYC EMD FB-7	189.95	____
(FB7004)	NP EMD FB-7	189.95	____
(FB7005)	PRR EMD FB-7, tuscan	189.95	____
(FB7006)	PRR EMD FB-7, green	189.95	____
(FB7007)	SP EMD FB-7	189.95	____
(FB7008)	UP EMD FB-7	189.95	____
(FP7000)	Undecorated EMD FP-7	189.95	____
(FP7001)	BN EMD FP-7	189.95	____
(FP7002)	GN EMD FP-7	189.95	____
(FP7003)	NYC EMD FP-7	189.95	____
(FP7004)	NP EMD FP-7	189.95	____
(FP7005)	PRR EMD FP-7, tuscan	189.95	____
(FP7006)	PRR EMD FP-7, green	189.95	____
(FP7007)	SP EMD FP-7	189.95	____
(FP7008)	UP EMD FP-7	189.95	____
(GG1200)	Undecorated GG-1 Electric	309.95	____
(GG1201)	PRR GG-1 Electric, green	309.95	____
(GG1202)	PRR GG-1 Electric, tuscan	309.95	____
(GP9000)	Undecorated EMD GP-9	189.95	____
(GP9001)	Conrail EMD GP-9	189.95	____
(GP9002)	Erie Lackawanna EMD GP-9	189.95	____
(GP9003)	NH EMD GP-9	189.95	____
(GP9004)	NYC EMD GP-18 "5918"	189.95	____
(GP9005)	N&W EMD GP-9	189.95	____
(GP9006)	PRR EMD GP-9	189.95	____
(GP9007)	ATSF EMD GP-9	189.95	____
(GP9008)	SP EMD GP-9	189.95	____
(GP9009)	UP EMD GP-9	189.95	____
(GP9010)	C&O EMD GP-9	189.95	____
(GGCC)	PRR GG-1 Electric, Congressional, Chrome	249.95	____
(GGCS)	PRR GG-1 Electric, Congressional, Silver	249.95	____
(GGGI)	PRR GG-1 Electric, Green, 1-Stripe	249.95	____
(GGGS)	PRR GG-1 Electric, Green, 5-Stripe	249.95	____
(GGR6)	PRR GG-1 Electric, Tuscan, 5-Stripe	249.95	____
(GGRI)	PRR GG-1 Electric, Tuscan, 1-Stripe	249.95	____
(GP35000)	Undecorated EMD GP-35	189.95	____
(GP35001)	C&O EMD GP-35	189.95	____
(GP35002)	CNW EMD GP-35	199.95	____
(GP35003)	Conrail EMD GP-35	199.95	____
(GP35004)	Erie Lackawanna EMD GP-35	189.95	____
(GP35005)	GN EMD GP-35	199.95	____
(GP35006)	MP EMD GP-35	189.95	____
(GP35007)	NYC EMD GP-35	189.95	____
(GP35008)	PRR EMD GP-35	189.95	____
(GP35010)	SP EMD GP-35	199.95	____
(GP35011)	UP EMD GP-35	199.95	____
(GP35012)	BN EMD GP-35	199.95	____

	Retail	Cond/$
(GP35013) CSX EMD GP-35	209.95	____
(GP35014) ATSF EMD GP-35, warbonnet	209.95	____
(GP35015) Soo Line EMD GP-35	189.95	____
(GP35016) D&RGW EMD GP-35	199.95	____
(GP35017) Ann Harbor EMD GP-35 "383"	189.95	____
(HA8000) Undecorated 80' Passenger Lightweight Streamline set	249.95	____
(HA8001) GN 80' Passenger Lightweight Streamline set	249.95	____
(HA8002) NP 80' Passenger Lightweight Streamline set	249.95	____
(HA8003) NYC 80' Passenger Lightweight Streamline set	249.95	____
(HA8004) PRR 80' Passenger Lightweight Streamline set	249.95	____
(HA8006) UP 80' Passenger Lightweight Streamline set	249.95	____
(HA8100) Undecorated Baggage-Dormitory	44.95	____
(HA8101) NP Baggage-Dormitory	44.95	____
(HA8103) NYC Baggage-Dormitory	44.95	____
(HA8104) PRR Baggage-Dormitory	44.95	____
(HA8106) UP Baggage-Dormitory	44.95	____
(HA8111) GN Baggage-Dormitory	44.95	____
(HA8200) Undecorated 60-seat Coach	44.95	____
(HA8201) NP 60-seat Coach	44.95	____
(HA8203) NYC 60-seat Coach	44.95	____
(HA8204) PRR 60-seat Coach	44.95	____
(HA8206) UP 60-seat Coach	44.95	____
(HA8211) GN 60-seat Coach	44.95	____
(HA8300) Undecorated Vista Dome	44.95	____
(HA8301) NP Vista Dome	44.95	____
(HA8303) NYC Vista Dome	44.95	____
(HA8304) PRR Vista Dome	44.95	____
(HA8306) UP Vista Dome	44.95	____
(HA8311) GN Vista Dome	44.95	____
(HA8400) Undecorated 4-16 Duplex Sleeper	44.95	____
(HA8401) NP 4-16 Duplex Sleeper	44.95	____
(HA8403) NYC 4-16 Duplex Sleeper	44.95	____
(HA8404) PRR 4-16 Duplex Sleeper	44.95	____
(HA8406) UP 4-16 Duplex Sleeper	44.95	____
(HA8411) GN 4-16 Duplex Sleeper	44.95	____
(HA8500) Undecorated Observation Lounge	44.95	____
(HA8501) NP Observation Lounge	44.95	____
(HA8503) NYC Observation Lounge	44.95	____
(HA8504) PRR Observation Lounge	44.95	____
(HA8506) UP Observation Lounge	44.95	____
(HA8511) GN Observation Lounge	44.95	____

	Retail	Cond/S
(HW8000) Undecorated 72' Heavyweight Passenger set	289.95	____
(HW8001) CNW 72' Heavyweight Passenger set	289.95	____
(HW8003) UP 72' Heavyweight Passenger set	289.95	____
(HW8004) NH 72' Heavyweight Passenger set	289.95	____
(HW8005) NYC 72' Heavyweight Passenger set	289.95	____
(HW8006) ATSF 72' Heavyweight Passenger set	289.95	____
(HW8007) D&RGW 72' Heavyweight Passenger set	289.95	____
(HW8008) C&NW 72' Heavyweight Passenger set	289.95	____
(HW8009) PRR 72' Heavyweight Passenger set	289.95	____
(HW8010) PRR 72' Heavyweight Passenger set w/ Pullman	289.95	____
(HW8012) SP 72' Heavyweight Passenger set	289.95	____
(HW8013) Pullman green Heavyweight car set, no lettering	289.95	____
(HW8014) Undecorated Pullman Green Heavyweight Passenger set (Green Roof)	289.95	____
(HW8200) Undecorated Heavyweight Coach	59.95	____
(HW8201) CNW Heavyweight Coach	59.95	____
(HW8203) UP Heavyweight Coach	59.95	____
(HW8204) NH Heavyweight Coach	59.95	____
(HW8205) NYC Heavyweight Coach	59.95	____
(HW8206) ATSF Heavyweight Coach	59.95	____
(HW8207) D&RGW Heavyweight Coach	59.95	____
(HW8209) PRR Heavyweight Coach	59.95	____
(HW8210) PRR Heavyweight Coach w/ Pullman	59.95	____
(HW8212) SP Heavyweight Coach	59.95	____
(HW8213) Undecorated Heavyweight Pullman (Black Roof)	59.95	____
(HX8100) Undecorated 80' Pullman Heavyweight 12-1 Sleeper	54.95	____
(HX8200) Undecorated 80' Pullman Heavyweight 10-1 Sleeper	54.95	____
(HX8300) Undecorated 80' Pullman Heavyweight Cafe	54.95	____
(J3a) NYC J3a-class Hudson 4-6-4 Steam Locomotive and Tender	349.95	____
(K46201AC) PRR K4 Torpedo, bronze	429.95	____
(K46202AC) PRR K4 Torpedo, green	429.95	____
(LTD RUN) Wisconsin Central EMD GP-35 "728"	219.95	____
(PABA400) Undecorated Alco PA-1 ABA set	549.95	____
(PABA401) PRR Alco PA-1 ABA set, freight scheme, green	549.95	____
(PABA402) ATSF Alco PA-1 ABA set, warbonnet scheme, tuscan	549.95	____
(PABA403) NYC Alco PA-1 ABA set	549.95	____
(PABA404) NYC Alco PA-2 ABA set	549.95	____
(PABA405) NYC System Alco PA-1 ABA set	549.95	____

		Retail	Cond/S
(PABA406)	D&RGW Alco PA-1 ABA set	549.95	____
(PABA407)	NH McGuiness scheme Alco PA-1 ABA set	549.95	____
(PABA408)	UP Alco PA-1 ABA set	549.95	____
(PABA409)	ATSF Alco PA-1 ABA set, warbonnet scheme	549.95	____
(PABA410)	ATSF Alco PA-1 ABA set, freight scheme	549.95	____
(PABA411)	D&H Alco PA-1 ABA set	549.95	____
(PABA412)	SP Daylight Alco PA-1 ABA set "6055"	584.95	____
(RS299.950)	Undecorated Alco RS-3	189.95	____
(RS299.951)	Conrail Alco RS-3	189.95	____
(RS299.952)	SSW/SP Alco RS-3	189.95	____
(RS299.953)	EL Alco RS-3	189.95	____
(RS299.954)	GN Alco RS-3	189.95	____
(RS299.955)	NH Alco RS-3	189.95	____
(RS299.956)	NYC Alco RS-3	189.95	____
(RS299.957)	PRR Alco RS-3	189.95	____
(RS3000)	Undecorated Alco RS-3	189.95	____
(RS3001)	Conrail Alco RS-3	189.95	____
(RS3002)	SSW/SP Alco RS-3	189.95	____
(RS3003)	EL Alco RS-3	189.95	____
(RS3004)	GN Alco RS-3	189.95	____
(RS3005)	NH Alco RS-3	189.95	____
(RS3006)	NYC Alco RS-3	189.95	____
(RS3007)	PRR Alco RS-3	189.95	____
(RS3014)	RI RS-3 Diesel	189.95	____
(S1200)	Undecorated Baldwin S-12	199.95	____
(S1201)	NH Baldwin S-12	209.95	____
(S1202)	CNW Baldwin S-12	209.95	____
(S1203)	Conrail Baldwin S-12	199.95	____
(S1204)	Erie Lackawanna Baldwin S-12	214.95	____
(S1205)	Erie Lackawanna Baldwin S-12	199.95	____
(S1206)	Southern Baldwin S-12	219.95	____
(S1207)	NYC Baldwin S-12	199.95	—
(S1208)	PRR Baldwin C 12	199.95	____
(S1209)	ATSF Baldwin S-12	214.95	____
(S1210)	SP Baldwin S-12	209.95	____
(S1211)	UP Baldwin S-12	209.95	____
(S1212)	DRG Baldwin S-12	214.95	____
(S1213)	DRG Baldwin S-12	199.95	____
(S1214)	CB&Q Baldwin S-12	214.95	____
(S1215)	BN Baldwin S-12	199.95	____
(S1216)	BN Baldwin S-12	199.95	____
(S1217)	BN Baldwin S-12	199.95	____
(S1218)	BN Baldwin S-12	199.95	____
(S1219)	B&O Baldwin S-12	199.95	____
(S1220)	IC Baldwin S-12	209.95	____
(S1221)	IC Baldwin S-12	199.95	____
(S1222)	CP Baldwin S-12	214.95	____

		Retail	Cond/$
(S1223)	CP Baldwin S-12	199.95	____
(S1224)	SP Baldwin S-12 "106"	214.95	____
(SC65T)	Trailer Train 5-unit Spine set w/ trailer	159.95	____
(SD6000)	Undecorated EMD SD60 Diesel (Long Nose)	249.95	____
(SD6000AA)	Undecorated. EMD SD60 Diesel AA (Long Nose)	449.95	____
(SD6000Low)	Undecorated EMD SD60 Diesel (Low Nose)	249.95	____
(SD6000LowAA)	Undecorated EMD SD60 Diesel AA (Low Nose)	449.95	____
(SD6000M)	Undecrated EMD SD60 Diesel (Wide Cab)	249.95	____
(SD6000MAA)	Undecorated EMD SD60 Diesel AA (Wide Cab)	449.95	____
(SD6002)	C&NW EMD SD60 Diesel (Long Nose)	249.95	____
(SD6002AA)	C&NW EMD SD60 Diesel AA (Long Nose)	449.95	____
(SD6003M)	Conrail EMD SD60 Diesel (Wide Cab)	249.95	____
(SD6003MAA)	Conrail EMD SD60 Diesel AA (Wide Cab)	449.95	____
(SD6011)	UP EMD SD60 Diesel (Long Nose)	249.95	____
(SD6011AA)	UP EMD SD60 Diesel AA (Long Nose)	449.95	____
(SD6011M)	UP EMD SD60 Diesel (Wide Cab)	249.95	____
(SD6011MAA)	UP EMD SD60 Diesel AA (Wide Cab)	449.95	____
(SD6012)	BN EMD SD60 Diesel (Long Nose)	249.95	____
(SD6012AA)	BN EMD SD60 Diesel AA (Long Nose)	449.95	____
(SD6012M)	BN EMD SD60 Diesel (Wide Cab)	249.95	____
(SD6012MAA)	BN EMD SD60 Diesel AA (Wide Cab)	449.95	____
(SD6013)	CSX EMD SD60 Diesel (Long Nose)	249.95	____
(SD6013AA)	CSX EMD SD60 Diesel AA (Long Nose)	449.95	____
(SD6013M)	CSX EMD SD60 Diesel (Wide Cab)	249.95	____
(SD6013MAA)	CSX EMD SD60 Diesel AA (Wide Cab)	449.95	____
(SD6015)	Soo Line EMD SD60 Diesel (Long Nose)	249.95	____
(SD6015AA)	Soo Line EMD SD60 Diesel AA (Long Nose)	449.95	____
(SD6015M)	Soo Line EMD SD60 Diesel (Wide Cab)	249.95	____
(SD6015MAA)	Soo Line EMD SD60 Diesel AA (Wide Cab)	449.95	____
(SD6024)	NS EMD SD60 Diesel (Long Nose)	249.95	____
(SD6024AA)	NS EMD SD60 Diesel AA (Long Nose)	449.95	____
(SD6025M)	BNSF EMD SD60 Diesel (Wide Cab)	249.95	____
(SD6025MAA)	BNSF EMD SD60 Diesel AA (Wide Cab)	449.95	____
(SD60EMD)	EMD SD60 Diesel (Long Nose)	249.95	____
(SD60EMDAA)	EMD SD60 Diesel AA (Long Nose)	449.95	____
(SLBSP2)	Amtrak Superliner set, Phase II	369.95	____
(SLBSP3)	Amtrak Superliner set, Phase III	369.95	____
(T-1)	UP 40' Semi Trailer "Trailer Freight Service"	11.95	____
(T-2)	SOU 40' Semi Trailer "700425"	11.95	____

		Retail	Cond/S
(T-3)	BN 40' Semi Trailer "BNZ 233304"	11.95	____
(T-4)	CSX 40' Semi Trailer "580Z231008"	11.95	____
(T-5)	D&RGW 40' Semi Trailer "RRGZ 201077"	11.95	____
(T-6)	AT&SF 40' Semi Trailer	11.95	____
(T-7)	SP 40' Semi Trailer	11.95	____
(T-8)	Quantum 40' Semi Trailer "HSFZ610007"	11.95	____
(T-9)	IC 40' Semi Trailer	11.95	____
(T-10)	CN&W 40' Semi Trailer	11.95	____
(T-11)	Conrail 40' Semi Trailer	11.95	____
(T-12)	American President Line 40' Semi Trailer	11.95	____
(T-13)	K-Line 40' Semi Trailer	11.95	____
(T-14)	Evergreen 40' Semi Trailer	11.95	____
(T-15)	N&W 40' Semi Trailer "TCSZ216380"	11.95	____
(T-16)	Transamerica 40' Semi Trailer "TDSZ500035"	11.95	____
(T-17)	MP 40' Semi Trailer "MPZ20322"	11.95	____
(T-18)	SP 40' Semi Trailer "SPLZ731908"	11.95	____
(T148L)	LH 27"-radius Track	17.98	____
(T148R)	RH 27"-radius Track	17.98	____
(T710)	Rail Joiners (36)	2.25	____
(T711)	Terminal w/ wire	1.50	____
(T14812)	12" Straight Track	2.98	____
(T14821)	21"-radius S-42 Track	3.08	____
(T14824)	24"-radius S-48 Track	3.28	____
(T14827)	27"-radius S-54 Track	3.28	____
(T148L-PW)	LH 27"-radius Turnout powered	34.95	____
(T148R-PW)	RH 27"-radius Turnout powered	34.95	____
(T148R-HT)	RH 27"-radius Turnout w/ hand throw	25.95	____
(T148L-HT)	LH 27"-radius Turnout w/ hand throw	25.95	____
(T148B)	Bumpers 2-pack	5.95	____
(T14836)	3' Flex Track	7.50	____
(TM00)	Undecorated FM H-24-66 Diesel	249.95	____
(TM01)	C&NW FM H-24-66 Diesel	249.95	____
(TM02)	Lackawanna FM H-24-66 Diesel	249.95	____
(TM03)	Pennsylvania FM H-24-66 Diesel	249.95	____
(TM04)	Reading FM H-24-66 Diesel	249.95	____
(TM05)	SP FM H-24-66 Diesel	249.95	____
(TM06)	Virginian FM H-24-66 Diesel	249.95	____
(TMC-L)	LH Turnout Powering Kit	13.95	____
(TMC-R)	RH Turnout Powering Kit	13.95	____
(TMD)	Demonstrator FM H-24-66 Diesel	249.95	____
(TML)	LH Turnout Motor Kit	8.95	____
(TMR)	RH Turnout Motor Kit	8.95	____
(TSP)	Throw Bar Spring	0.50	____
(TWS103)	Rail Weathering Solution (3 oz.)	5.95	____

S-HELPER SERVICE
1994–2004

		Retail	Cond/$
(00001)	70-ton FB truck, code 110, *94-98, 02-03*	5.95	____
(00002)	70-ton FB truck, hi-rail, *94-98, 02-03*	5.95	____
(00003)	70-ton RB truck, code 110, *94-98, 02-03*	5.95	____
(00004)	70-ton RB truck, hi-rail, *94-98, 02-03*	5.95	____
(00005)	Hi-rail Freight Coupler, pair, *94-98, 02-03*	2.95	____
(00006)	B&M PS-2 Covered Hopper, "5541", *94-95*	39.95	____
(00007)	NYC PS-2 Covered Hopper, "573251", *94-95*	39.95	____
(00008)	PRR PS-2 Covered Hopper, "257701", *94-95*	39.95	____
(00009)	SF PS-2 Covered Hopper, "87421", *94-95*	39.95	____
(00010)	Wabash PS-2 Covered Hopper, "30321", *94-95*	39.95	____
(00011)	WM PS-2 Covered Hopper, "5531", *94-95*	39.95	____
(00012)	BN PS-2 Covered Hopper, "42471", *94-95*	39.95	____
(00013)	Chessie-WM PS-2 Covered Hopper, "5861", *94-95*	39.95	____
(00014)	CNW PS-2 Covered Hopper, "70551", *94-95*	39.95	____
(00015)	Conrail PS-2 Covered Hopper, "877351", *94-95*	39.95	____
(00016)	Soo Line PS-2 Covered Hopper, "69091", *94-95*	39.95	____
(00017)	SP PS-2 Covered Hopper, "401431", *94-96*	39.95	____
(00018)	CNJPS-2 Covered Hopper, "751", *94-96*	39.95	____
(00019)	MILW PS-2 Covered Hopper, "99631", *94-96*	39.95	____
(00020)	Trona PS-2 Covered Hopper, "31053", *94*	39.95	____
(00021)	Unlettered PS-2 Covered Hopper, friction bearing, gray, *94-96*	39.95	____
(00022)	PRR PS-2 Covered Hopper, "257781", *94-95*	39.95	____
(00023)	S-2 70-ton RB truck w/ 36" Wheels, Code 110, *94-98, 02-03*	6.50	____
(00024)	33" Scale Wheelsets, 4-pack, *94-98, 02-03*	3.95	____
(00025)	33" Hi-rail Wheelsets, 4-pack, *94-98, 03*	3.95	____
(00026)	PRR PS-2 Covered Hopper, "257862", sm. keystone, *94*	39.95	____
(00027)	B&O PS-2 Covered Hopper, "631512", *95-96*	39.95	____
(00028)	D&RGW PS-2 Covered Hopper, "18332", *95-96*	39.95	____
(00029)	SF PS-2 Covered Hopper, "82412", scheme #2, *95-96*	39.95	____
(00030)	MEC PS-2 Covered Hopper, "2492", *95-96, 02*	39.95	____
(00031)	UP PS-2 Covered Hopper, "11561", *95-96*	39.95	____
(00032)	WC PS-2 Covered Hopper, "81152", *95-96*	39.95	____
(00033)	LV PS-2 Covered Hopper, "50772", *95-96*	39.95	____
(00034)	RI PS-2 Covered Hopper, "507102", scheme #1, *95*	39.95	____
(00035)	RI PS-2 Covered Hopper, "507182", scheme #2, *95*	39.95	____
(00036)	DT&I PS-2 Covered Hopper, "11186", *95-96*	39.95	____
(00037)	CSX PS-2 Covered Hopper, "22606L", *95-96*	39.95	____
(00038)	CNW/CNW PS-2 Covered Hopper, "95242", scheme #2, *95*	39.95	____

(00039)	CNW/CGW PS-2 Covered Hopper, "7232", *95*	39.95	____
(00040)	BN PS-2 Covered Hopper, "424702", *95*	39.95	____
(00041)	DT&I PS-2 Covered Hopper, "11196", scheme #2, *95-96*	39.95	____
(00042)	IMCO PS-2 Covered Hopper, "41012", *95*	39.95	____
(00043)	Unlettered PS-2 Covered Hopper, roller bearing, gray, *95*	39.95	____
(00044)	Chessie/B&O PS-2 Covered Hopper, "631542", *95-96*	39.95	____
(00045)	50-ton Andrews Truck, code 110, *96-98, 02*	5.95	____
(00046)	50-ton Andrews Truck, hi-rail, *96-98, 02*	5.95	____
(00047)	50-ton 2D-F8 Truck, code 110, *96-98, 02*	5.95	____
(00048)	50-ton 2D-F8 Truck, hi-rail, *96-98, 02*	5.95	____
(00049)	Unlettered Stock Car, red, *96*	39.95	____
(00050)	UP Stock Car, "49001", scheme #1, *96*	39.95	____
(00051)	UP Stock Car, "49042", scheme #2, *96*	39.95	____
(00052)	Rio Grande Stock Car, "36491", *96*	39.95	____
(00053)	CNW Stock Car, "14201", scheme #1, *96*	39.95	____
(00054)	CNW Stock Car, "14252", scheme #2, *96*	39.95	____
(00055)	ACL Stock Car, "140441", *96, 02*	39.95	____
(00056)	GN Stock Car, "53051", scheme #1, *96*	39.95	____
(00057)	GN Stock Car, "53083", scheme #2, *96*	39.95	____
(00058)	PRR Stock Car, "1218121", scheme #1, *96*	39.95	____
(00059)	PRR Stock Car, "1219172", scheme #2, *96*	39.95	____
(00060)	SF Stock Car, "23001", scheme #1, *96*	39.95	____
(00061)	SF Stock Car, "23062", scheme #2, *96*	39.95	____
(00062)	NP Stock Car, "24001", *96*	39.95	____
(00063)	Unlettered USRA Wooden Boxcar, red, *96*	39.95	____
(00064)	NYC Stock Car, "22591", *96*	39.95	____
(00065)	WP Stock Car, "75891", *96*	39.95	____
(00066)	PRR USRA Wooden Boxcar, "564281", #1, *96*	39.95	____
(00067)	PRR USRA Wooden Boxcar, "518392", #2, *96*	39.95	____
(00068)	CB&Q/C&S USRA Wooden Boxcar, "13501", *96*	39.95	____
(00069)	CB&Q/CB&Q USRA Wooden Boxcar, "25321", *96*	39.95	____
(00070)	MEC/PTM USRA Wooden Boxcar, "2081", *96*	39.95	____
(00071)	B&O USRA Wooden Boxcar, "167051", *96*	39.95	____
(00072)	SP USRA Wooden Boxcar, "26541", *96*	39.95	____
(00073)	NYC USRA Wooden Boxcar, "277361", *96*	39.95	____
(00074)	NMRA-GG, YV&N USRA Wooden Boxcar, "77569", *96*	39.95	____
(00075)	CP USRA Wooden Boxcar, "230471", *96*	39.95	____
(00076)	GN PS-2 Covered Hopper, "71451", *96, 02*	39.95	____
(00077)	NKP PS-2 Covered Hopper, "905003", *96*	39.95	____
(00078)	PL&E (NYC) PS-2 Covered Hopper, "1563", *96, 02*	39.95	____
(00079)	Soo Line PS-2 Covered Hopper, "6873", scheme #2, *96, 02*	39.95	____
(00080)	New Haven PS-2 Covered Hopper, "117093", *96, 03*	39.95	____
(00081)	WP PS-2 Covered Hopper, "11203", *96*	39.95	____

		Retail	Cond/$
(00082)	MKT PS-2 Covered Hopper, "1333", *96, 02*	39.95	____
(00083)	BN PS-2 Covered Hopper, "424723", *96*	39.95	____
(00084)	PC PS-2 Covered Hopper, "74202", *96, 02*	39.95	____
(00085)	Chessie (CSXT) PS-2 Covered Hopper, "226403", *96*	39.95	____
(00086)	CNW/CNW PS-2 Covered Hopper, "69473", *96*	39.95	____
(00087)	Revere Sugar PS-2 Covered Hopper, "133", *96*	39.95	____
(00088)	Conrail PS-2 Covered Hopper, "877353", scheme #2, *96, 02*	39.95	____
(00089)	Grand Trunk PS-2 Covered Hopper, "111163", *96*	39.95	____
(00090)	Ready Mix Concrete PS-2 Covered Hopper, "326", *96*	39.95	____
(00091)	SP PS-2 Covered Hopper, "402243" scheme #2, *96, 02*	39.95	____
(00092)	Unlettered SW-9, black, *97*	199.95	____
(00093)	ACL SW-9, "701", scheme #1, *97*	199.95	____
(00094)	ACL SW-9 "652", scheme #2, *97*	199.95	____
(00095)	Amtrak SW-9, scheme #1, *97*	199.95	____
(00096)	Amtrak SW-9, scheme #2, *97*	199.95	____
(00097)	B&O SW-9 "9611", scheme #1, *97*	199.95	____
(00098)	B&O SW-9 "9612", scheme #2, *97*	199.95	____
(00099)	B&M SW-9 "1231", scheme #1, *97*	199.95	____
(00100)	B&M SW-9 "1222", scheme #2, *97*	199.95	____
(00101)	BN SW-9 "161", scheme #1, *97*	199.95	____
(00102)	BN SW-9 "169", scheme #2, *97*	199.95	____
(00103)	CP SW-9 "7401", scheme #1, *97-03*	199.95	____
(00104)	CP SW-9 "7405", scheme #2, *97-03*	199.95	____
(00105)	CB&Q SW-9 "9269", scheme #1, *97*	199.95	____
(00106)	CB&Q SW-9 "9270", scheme #2, *97*	199.95	____
(00107)	Chessie System SW-9 "C&O", scheme #1, *97*	199.95	____
(00108)	Chessie System SW-9 "WM", scheme #2, *97*	199.95	____
(00109)	CNW SW-9 "1101", scheme #1, *97*	199.95	____
(00110)	CNW SW-9 "1102", scheme #2, *97*	199.95	____
(00111)	Conrail SW-9, scheme #1, *97*	199.95	____
(00112)	Conrail SW-9, scheme #2, *97*	199.95	____
(00113)	Erie Lack. SW-9 "451", scheme #1, *97*	199.95	____
(00114)	Erie Lack. SW-9 "452", scheme #2, *97*	199.95	____
(00115)	NYC SW-9 "8971", scheme #1, *97*	199.95	____
(00116)	NYC SW-9 "8922", scheme #2, *97*	199.95	____
(00117)	PRR SW-9 "8531", scheme #1, *97*	199.95	____
(00118)	PRR SW-9 "8522", scheme #2, *97*	199.95	____
(00119)	SF SW-9 "2421", scheme #1, *97*	199.95	____
(00120)	SF SW-9 "2432", scheme #2, *97*	199.95	____
(00121)	UP SW-9 "1841", scheme #1, *97*	199.95	____
(00122)	UP SW-9 "1862", scheme #2, *97*	199.95	____
(00123)	UP Stock Car, scheme #3, *97*	39.95	____
(00124)	Unlettered Rebuilt, red, *97*	39.95	____
(00125)	C&O Rebuilt "12681", *97*	39.95	____
(00126)	CNW Rebuilt, *97*	39.95	____
(00127)	DL&W Rebuilt "48001", *97*	39.95	____
(00128)	Frisco Rebuilt "128011", *97*	39.95	____
(00129)	NYC Rebuilt, *97*	39.95	____

		Retail	Cond/$
(00130)	NYC/PMKY Rebuilt "83401", *97*	39.95	___
(00131)	PRR #1 Rebuilt, *97*	39.95	___
(00132)	PRR #2 Rebuilt, *97*	39.95	___
(00133)	SF #1 Rebuilt, *97*	39.95	___
(00134)	SF #2 Rebuilt, *97*	39.95	___
(00135)	VC Rebuilt, *97*	39.95	___
(00136)	CN Stock Car "810522", *97*	39.95	___
(00137)	CB&Q Stock Car "52881", *97*	39.95	___
(00138)	MP Stock Car "154092", *97, 02*	39.95	___
(00139)	MKT Stock Car "47021", *97*	39.95	___
(00140)	UP Stock Car "0SL39193", *97*	39.95	___
(00141)	Rutland USRA Wooden Boxcar, *97*	39.95	___
(00142)	Clinchfield USRA Wooden Boxcar "8051", *97, 02*	39.95	___
(00143)	Erie USRA Wooden Boxcar, *97, 02*	39.95	___
(00144)	MILW USRA Wooden Boxcar, *97*	39.95	___
(00145)	PRR-MOW USRA Wooden Boxcar, *97*	39.95	___
(00146)	USRA Wooden Boxcar, *97-03*	39.95	___
(00147)	Wabash USRA Wooden Boxcar, *97, 02*	39.95	___
(00148)	Chessie/B&O SW-9 Diesel Switcher " B&O 9602", *97-98*	199.95	___
(00149)	CN 40' Stock Car "810371", *97-98, 02*	39.95	___
(00150)	CB&Q 40' Stock Car "52251", *97-98*	39.95	___
(00151)	MKT 40' Stock Car "47372", *97-98*	39.95	___
(00152)	UP/OSL 40' Stock Car "39341", scheme #2, *97-98, 02*	39.95	___
(00153)	C&O 40' Rebuilt Steel Boxcar "12684", *97*	39.95	___
(00154)	Frisco 40' Rebuilt Steel Boxcar "128000", *97*	39.95	___
(00155)	Unlettered 53'6" Bulkhead Flatcar, *97-98*	49.95	___
(00156)	BN 53'6" Bulkhead Flatcar "629091", scheme #1, *97-98*	49.95	___
(00157)	BN 53'6" Bulkhead Flatcar "629052", scheme #2, *97-98*	49.95	___
(00158)	CB&Q 53'6" Bulkhead Flatcar "95221", scheme #2, *97-98, 02*	49.95	___
(00159)	CB&Q 53'6" Bulkhead Flatcar "95282", scheme #1, *97-98, 02*	49.95	___
(00160)	D&RGW 53'6" Bulkhead Flatcar "22761", *97-98, 02*	49.95	___
(00161)	IC 53'6" Bulkhead Flatcar "92641", scheme #1, *97-98, 02*	49.95	___
(00162)	IC 53'6" Bulkhead Flatcar "92642", scheme #2, *97-98*	49.95	___
(00163)	SOU 53'6" Bulkhead Flatcar "51861", *97-98, 02*	49.95	___
(00164)	UP 53'6" Bulkhead Flatcar "15061", scheme #1, *97-98*	49.95	___
(00165)	UP 53'6" Bulkhead Flatcar "15082", scheme #2, *97-98*	49.95	___
(00166)	Wabash 53'6" Bulkhead Flatcar "181", *97-98*	49.95	___
(00167)	Unlettered 53'6" Standard Flatcar, *97-98*	39.95	___
(00168)	Unlettered 53'6" Standard Flatcar, *97-98*	39.95	___

		Retail	Cond/$
(00169)	BN 53'6" Standard Flatcar "629091", *97-98*	39.95	____
(00170)	CB&Q 53'6" Standard Flatcar "95221", *97-98*	39.95	____
(00171)	D&RGW 53'6" Standard Flatcar "22761", *97-98*	39.95	____
(00172)	IC 53'6" Standard Flatcar "92641", *97-98*	39.95	____
(00173)	SOU 53'6" Standard Flatcar "51861", *97-98*	39.95	____
(00174)	UP 53'6" Standard Flatcar "15061", *97-98*	39.95	____
(00175)	Wabash 53'6" Standard Flatcar "181", *97-98*	39.95	____
(00176)	PRR 53'6" Standard Flatcar "469997", *97-98*	39.95	____
(00177)	Unlettered 53'6" Trailer on Flatcar, *97-98*	59.95	____
(00178)	B&A 53'6" Trailer on Flatcar "451", *97-98, 02*	59.95	____
(00179)	NKP 53'6" Trailer on Flatcar "3021", *97-98, 02*	59.95	____
(00180)	RI 53'6" Trailer on Flatcar "90991", *97-98, 02*	59.95	____
(00181)	PRR 53'6" Trailer on Flatcar "92761", scheme #1, *97-98, 02*	59.95	____
(00182)	PRR 53'6" Trailer on Flatcar "92762", scheme #2, *97-98, 02*	59.95	____
(00183)	Seaboard 53'6" Trailer on Flatcar "47101", *97-98*	59.95	____
(00184)	UP 53'6" Trailer on Flatcar "15321", scheme #1, *97-98, 02*	59.95	____
(00185)	UP 53'6" Trailer on Flatcar "15322", scheme #2, *97-98, 02*	59.95	____
(00186)	Unlettered 53'6" Trailer on Flatcar, *97-98*	59.95	____
(00187)	C&NW 53'6" Trailer on Flatcar "44151", *97-98, 02*	59.95	____
(00188)	C&NW 53'6" Trailer on Flatcar "44152", *97-98, 02*	59.95	____
(00189)	NH 53'6" Trailer on Flatcar "17341", scheme #1, *97-98, 02*	59.95	____
(00190)	NH 53'6" Trailer on Flatcar "17382", scheme #2, *97-98, 02*	59.95	____
(00191)	NYC 53'6" Trailer on Flatcar "499701", scheme #1, *97-98, 02*	59.95	____
(00192)	NYC 53'6" Trailer on Flatcar "499612", scheme #2, *97-98, 02*	59.95	____
(00193)	TTX/REAX 53'6" Trailer on Flatcar "475001", *97-98*	59.95	____
(00194)	TTX/REAX 53'6" Trailer on Flatcar "475002", *97-98, 02*	59.95	____
(00195)	Unlettered 35' Horizontal Corr. Trailer, *97-98*	15.95	____
(00196)	Unlettered 35' Vertical Post Trailer, *97-98*	15.95	____
(00197)	B&A 35' Horizontal Corr. Trailer, *97-98*	15.95	____
(00198)	NKP 35' Horizontal Corr. Trailer, *97-98*	15.95	____
(00199)	RI 35' Horizontal Corr. Trailer, *97-98*	15.95	____
(00200)	PRR 35' Horizontal Corr. Trailer, *97-98*	15.95	____
(00201)	Seaboard 35' Horizontal Corr. Trailer, *97-98*	15.95	____
(00202)	UP 35' Horizontal Corr. Trailer, *97-98*	15.95	____
(00203)	C&NW 35' Vertical Post Trailer, *97-98*	15.95	____
(00204)	NH 35' Vertical Post Trailer, *97-98*	15.95	____
(00205)	NYC 35' Vertical Post Trailer, *97-98*	15.95	____
(00206)	REA 35' Vertical Post Trailer, scheme #1, *97-98*	15.95	____
(00207)	REA 35' Vertical Post Trailer, scheme #2, *97-98*	15.95	____

		Retail	Cond/S
(00208)	B&A 53'6" Standard Flatcar "451", *97-98*	39.95	____
(00209)	C&NW 53'6" Standard Flatcar "44151", *97-98*	39.95	____
(00210)	NH 53'6" Standard Flatcar "17341", *97-98*	39.95	____
(00211)	NYC 53'6" Standard Flatcar "499701", *97-98*	39.95	____
(00212)	NKP 53'6" Standard Flatcar "3021", *97-98*	39.95	____
(00213)	PRR 53'6" Standard Flatcar "92761", *97-98*	39.95	____
(00214)	RI 53'6" Standard Flatcar "90991", *97-98*	39.95	____
(00215)	Seaboard 53'6" Standard Flatcar "47101", *97-98*	39.95	____
(00216)	UP 53'6" Standard Flatcar "15321", *97-98*	39.95	____
(00217)	Unlettered Wide Vision Caboose, *98*	69.95	____
(00218)	BN Wide Vision Caboose, scheme #1, *98-03*	69.95	____
(00219)	BN Wide Vision Caboose, scheme #2, *98-03*	69.95	____
(00220)	C&O Wide Vision Caboose, scheme #1, *98-02*	69.95	____
(00221)	C&O Wide Vision Caboose, scheme #2, *98*	69.95	____
(00222)	CB&Q Wide Vision Caboose, scheme #1, *98-03*	69.95	____
(00223)	CB&Q Wide Vision Caboose, scheme #2, *98-03*	69.95	____
(00224)	CSX Wide Vision Caboose, scheme #1, *98*	69.95	____
(00225)	CSX Wide Vision Caboose, scheme #2, *98*	69.95	____
(00226)	C&NW Wide Vision Caboose, scheme #1, *98*	69.95	____
(00227)	C&NW Wide Vision Caboose, scheme #2, *98*	69.95	____
(00228)	Conrail Wide Vision Caboose, scheme #1, *98*	69.95	____
(00229)	Conrail Wide Vision Caboose, scheme #2, *98*	69.95	____
(00230)	D&RGW Wide Vision Caboose, scheme #1, *98*	69.95	____
(00231)	D&RGW Wide Vision Caboose, scheme #1, *98*	69.95	____
(00232)	GN Wide Vision Caboose, scheme #1, *98*	69.95	____
(00233)	GN Wide Vision Caboose, scheme #2, *98-02*	69.95	____
(00234)	IC Wide Vision Caboose, scheme #1, *98-03*	69.95	____
(00235)	IC Wide Vision Caboose, scheme #2, *98-03*	69.95	____
(00236)	MP Wide Vision Caboose, scheme #1, *98-03*	69.95	____
(00237)	MP Wide Vision Caboose, scheme #2, *98-03*	69.95	____
(00238)	NP Wide Vision Caboose, scheme #1, *98-03*	69.95	____
(00239)	NP Wide Vision Caboose, scheme #2, *98-02*	69.95	____
(00240)	AT&SF Wide Vision Caboose, scheme #1, *98*	69.95	____
(00241)	AT&SF Wide Vision Caboose, scheme #2, *98*	69.95	____
(00242)	Seaboard Wide Vision Caboose, scheme #1, *98-03*	69.95	____
(00243)	Seaboard Wide Vision Caboose, scheme #2, *98-03*	69.95	____
(00244)	SOO Line Wide Vision Caboose, scheme #1, *98-02*	69.95	____
(00245)	SOO Line Wide Vision Caboose, scheme #2, *98-03*	69.95	____
(00246)	Evans Building Materials Load, *97-98, 03*	9.95	____
(00247)	Gold Bond Building Material Load, white, *97-98*	9.95	____
(00248)	Gold Bond Building Material Load, red, *97-98*	9.95	____
(00249)	Johns Manville Building Material Load, *97-98*	9.95	____
(00250)	Masonite Building Material Load, *97-98*	9.95	____
(00251)	Plumb Creek Building Material Load, *97-98*	9.95	____
(00252)	United States Gypsum Building Material Load, *97-98*	9.95	____

		Retail	Cond/S
(00253)	155# Rail Joiner/Connector, 12/pkg, *98-03*	4.95	____
(00254)	155# Rail Insulated Joiner/Connector, 12/pkg, *98-03*	2.95	____
(00255)	155# Rail Joiner/Connector w/ feeder wire, 12/pkg, *98-03*	7.95	____
(00256)	155#NS Track set, 20" radius, 16 pieces, *98-03*	69.95	____
(00257)	155#NS 15" Straight Track, 6/box, *98-03*	36.95	____
(00258)	155#NS 10" Straight Track, 6/box, *98-03*	29.95	____
(00259)	155#NS Curved Track, 20" radius, 30°, 6/box, *98-03*	29.95	____
(00260)	BN 53'6" Standard Flatcar "629052", scheme #2, *97-98*	39.95	____
(00261)	UP 53'6" Standard Flatcar "15082", scheme #2, *97-98*	39.95	____
(00262)	B&M 53'6" Trailer on Flatcar, "5205", 1998 NASG Conv. Car, *98*	59.95	____
(00263)	B&M 53'6" Standard Flatcar, "5202", *98*	39.95	____
(00264)	B&M 35' Vert. Post Trailer, "150", 1998 NASG Conv. Car, *98*	15.95	____
(00265)	36" Scale Wheelsets 4-pack, *94-99, 02*	3.95	____
(00266)	Milwaukee Road #1 Wide Vision Caboose, "992301", *98, 02*	69.95	____
(00267)	Milwaukee Road #2 Wide Vision Caboose, "992302", *98, 02*	69.95	____
(00268)	MEC Wide Vision Caboose, "671", 1998 Christmas Cab, *98*	69.95	____
(00269)	Montana Rail Link #1 Wide Vision Caboose	69.95	____
(00270)	Montana Rail Link #2 Wide Vision Caboose	69.95	____
(00271)	Unlettered-FB 3-bay Covered Hopper, *99*	39.95	____
(00272)	AT&SF (GA-90) 3-bay Covered Hopper, "300171", *99, 02*	39.95	____
(00273)	BN 3-bay Covered Hopper, *99*	39.95	____
(00274)	Chessie 3-bay Covered Hopper, "B&O 628031", *99*	39.95	____
(00275)	CB&Q 3-bay Covered Hopper, "85021", *99*	39.95	____
(00276)	C&NW 3-bay Covered Hopper, "435041", *99*	39.95	____
(00277)	Conrail 3-bay Covered Hopper, "883581", *99, 02*	39.95	____
(00278)	GN 3-bay Covered Hopper, "71971", *99*	39.95	____
(00279)	Erie Lackawanna 3-bay Covered Hopper, "21801", *99, 02*	39.95	____
(00280)	NYC 3-bay Covered Hopper, "883051", *99, 02*	39.95	____
(00281)	UP 3-bay Covered Hopper, "1921", *99, 02*	39.95	____
(00282)	C&NW/MStL (2) 2-bay Covered Hopper, *99, 02*	39.95	____
(00283)	Jack Frost 2-bay Covered Hopper, *99*	39.95	____
(00284)	LNE 2-bay Covered Hopper, "18101-200", *99, 02*	39.95	____
(00285)	MStL (NASG) 2-bay Covered Hopper, "70401-599", *99, 02*	39.95	____
(00286)	CSX (Central Soya) 2-bay Covered Hopper, "145-159", *99, 02*	39.95	____

		Retail	Cond/$
(00287)	NAHX (poly-borate) #1, 2-bay Covered Hopper, "31067", *99*	39.95	___
(00288)	NAHX (poly-borate) #2, 2-bay Covered Hopper, "31067", *99*	39.95	___
(00289)	Engineer & Fireman, Painted Seated Figures, *98, 02*	5.95	___
(00290)	AC/DC Rev Unit w/ DCC SOC Diesel Part, *98, 02*	249.95	___
(00291)	S-19 Radius 15° Curved Track, 6/box, *98-03*	26.95	___
(00292)	S-24 Radius 30° Curved Track, 6/box, *99-03*	34.95	___
(00293)	S-24 Radius 15° Curved Track, 6/box, *99-03*	27.95	___
(00294)	S-29 Radius 30° Curved Track, 6/box, *99-03*	36.95	___
(00295)	SW-9 coupler, AF-compatible, pair, *98, 03*	3.95	___
(00296)	29"-Radius 15° Curve (6), *03*	CP	___
(00297)	5" Straight Track 6/box, *99-03*	24.95	___
(00298)	RC Switches #3 RH Track, *01-03*	CP	___
(00299)	RC Switcher #3 LH Track, *01-03*	CP	___
(00300)	AT&SF 53'6" Trailer on Flatcar, "92752", *98*	59.95	___
(00301)	B&O 53'6" Trailer on Flatcar, "8742", *98*	59.95	___
(00302)	Maine Central 53'6" Bulkhead Flatcar, "7712", *99, 02*	49.95	___
(00303)	CP/Speedway 53'6" Trailer on Flatcar, "505012", *98, 02*	59.95	___
(00304)	GN 53'6" Trailer on Flatcar, "60242", *98*	59.95	___
(00305)	NH/Yale 53'6" Trailer on Flatcar, "17343", *98, 02*	59.95	___
(00306)	PRR 53'6" Trailer on Flatcar, "92763", *98, 02*	59.95	___
(00307)	TTX/Carolina 53'6" Trailer on Flatcar, "475083", *98, 02*	59.95	___
(00308)	Rio Grande 53'6" Trailer on Flatcar, "500002", *98*	59.95	___
(00309)	UP 53'6" Standard Flatcar w/ excavator, "58073", *98*	39.95	___
(00310)	WM 53'6" Trailer on Flatcar, "7002", *98, 02*	59.95	___
(00311)	AT&SF 53'6" Standard Flatcar, "92752", *98*	39.95	___
(00312)	B&O 53'6" Standard Flatcar, "8742", *99*	39.95	___
(00313)	Maine Central 53'6" Standard Flatcar, "7712", *99*	39.95	___
(00314)	CP 53'6" Standard Flatcar, "505012", *98*	39.95	___
(00315)	GN 53'6" Standard Flatcar, "60062", *98*	39.95	___
(00316)	NH #3 53'6" Standard Flatcar, "17343", *98*	39.95	___
(00317)	PRR #3 53'6" Standard Flatcar, "92763", *98*	39.95	___
(00318)	D&RGW 53'6" Standard Flatcar, "500002", *98*	39.95	___
(00319)	UP #4 53'6" Standard Flatcar	39.95	___
(00320)	WM 53'6" Standard Flatcar, "7002", *98*	39.95	___
(00321)	AT&SF 35' Horizontal Corr. Trailer, *98*	15.95	___
(00322)	B&O 35' Horizontal Corr. Trailer, *99*	15.95	___
(00323)	Speedway 35' Horizontal Corr. Trailer, *98*	15.95	___
(00324)	GN 35' Horizontal Corr. Trailer, "G322", *98*	15.95	___
(00325)	Yale 35' Vert. Post Trailer, *98*	15.95	___
(00326)	PRR 35' Vert. Post Trailer, *98*	15.95	___
(00327)	Carolina 35' Vert. Post Trailer, *98*	15.95	___

		Retail	Cond/S
(00328)	D&RGW 35' Horizontal Post Trailer, *98*	15.95	____
(00329)	UP #2 35' Horizontal Corr. Trailer	15.95	____
(00330)	WM 35' Vert. Post Trailer, *98*	15.95	____
(00331)	AT&SF #1 53'6" Bulkhead Flatcar, *98, 02*	49.95	____
(00332)	AT&SF #2 53'6" Bulkhead Flatcar, *98, 02*	49.95	____
(00333)	GN #1 53'6" Bulkhead Flatcar, "60342", *98, 02*	49.95	____
(00334)	GN #2 53'6" Bulkhead Flatcar, "60403", *98*	49.95	____
(00335)	Soo Line #1 53'6" Bulkhead Flatcar, "5573", *98, 02*	49.95	____
(00336)	Soo Line #2 53'6" Bulkhead Flatcar, *98, 02*	49.95	____
(00337)	D&H 53'6" Bulkhead Flatcar "16502", *97-98*	49.95	____
(00338)	WM/Chessie 53'6" Bulkhead Flatcar "WM 402", *97-98*	39.95	____
(00339)	Santa Fe #2 53'6" Standard Flatcar, *97-98*	39.95	____
(00340)	Great Northern #2 53'6" Standard Flatcar, "60403", *97-98*	39.95	____
(00341)	Soo Line #2 53'6" Standard Flatcar, "5573", *97-98*	39.95	____
(00342)	Delaware & Hudson 53'6" Standard Flatcar, "16502", *97-98*	39.95	____
(00343)	WM/Chessie 53'6" Standard Flatcar, "WM 402", *97-98*	39.95	____
(00344)	Santa Fe 3-car set, *97-98, 02*	99.95	____
(00345)	C&NW 3-car set, *97-98*	99.95	____
(00346)	GN #1 40' Rebuilt Steel Boxcar, "27001", *97-98*	39.95	____
(00347)	GN #2 40' Rebuilt Steel Boxcar, "27792", *97-98*	39.95	____
(00348)	MoPac #2 40' Rebuilt Steel Boxcar, *99*	39.95	____
(00349)	MoPac #1 40' Rebuilt Steel Boxcar, *99*	39.95	____
(00350)	NYC 3-car set, *99, 02*	99.95	____
(00351)	RS&P 40' Rebuilt Steel Boxcar, *99*	39.95	____
(00352)	UP 3-car set, *99, 02*	99.95	____
(00353)	Ball Lines 40' Rebuilt Steel Boxcar, *99*	39.95	____
(00354)	Gear Box, AF Comp Drivers, *98*	9.95	____
(00355)	Gear Box, Code 110 Drivers, *98*	9.95	____
(00356)	DCC Socket/DC Plug/AC pcb, *98*	39.95	____
(00357)	SW-9 Coupler, AF-compatible, bulk, *98*	3.95	____
(00358)	Conductor and Brakeman, painted fgures (seated), *98*	5.95	____
(00359)	EVC Coupler, AF-compatible, pair, *98, 02*	2.95	____
(00360)	10" Straight Track, Steel Rail, bulk	CP	____
(00361)	S-19, 30" Straight Track, Steel Rail, bulk	CP	____
(00362)	B&O #1, Diesel Cab, A&B set, "82", *99-03*	499.95	____
(00363)	B&O #2, Diesel Cab, A&B set, "84", *99-03*	499.95	____
(00364)	CB&Q #1, Diesel Cab, A&B set, "161", *99-03*	499.95	____
(00365)	CB&Q #2, Diesel Cab, A&B set, "162", *99-03*	499.95	____
(00366)	C&NW #1, Diesel Cab, A&B set, "201", *99-03*	499.95	____
(00367)	C&NW #2, Diesel Cab, A&B set, "201", *99-03*	499.95	____
(00368)	DL&W #1, Diesel Cab, A&B set, "803A-B", *99-03*	499.95	____
(00369)	DL&W #2, Diesel Cab, A&B set, "805A-B", *99-03*	499.95	____

		Retail	Cond/S
(00370)	Maine Central #1, Diesel Cab, A&B set, "671", *99-03*	499.95	____
(00371)	Maine Central #2, Diesel Cab, A&B set, "672", *99-03*	499.95	____
(00372)	NYC #1, Diesel Cab, A&B set, "3501", *99-03*	499.95	____
(00373)	NYC #2, Diesel Cab, A&B set, "3502", *99-03*	499.95	____
(00374)	Southern #1, Diesel Cab, A&B set, "4171/4353", *99-03*	499.95	____
(00375)	Southern #2, Diesel Cab, A&B set, "4172/4354", *99-03*	499.95	
(00376)	SP #1, Diesel Cab, A&B set, "6100s", *99-03*	499.95	____
(00377)	SP #2, Diesel Cab, A&B set, "6100s", *99-03*	499.95	____
(00378)	UP #1, Diesel Cab, A&B set, "1400s", *99-03*	499.95	____
(00379)	UP #2, Diesel Cab, A&B set, "1400s", *99-03*	499.95	____
(00380)	WP #1, Diesel Cab, A&B set, "801", *99-02*	499.95	____
(00381)	WP #2, Diesel Cab, A&B set, "802", *99-03*	499.95	____
(00382)	Undecorated, Diesel Cab, A&B set, *99*	499.95	____
(00383)	Barber EVC, RB Code 110 Truck, *98, 02*	9.95	____
(00384)	Barber EVC, RB AF-compatible Truck, *98, 02*	9.95	____
(00385)	NYC Frt. #1, Diesel Cab, A&B set, "1600s", *99*	499.95	____
(00386)	NYC Frt. #2, Diesel Cab, A&B set, "1600s", *99*	499.95	____
(00387)	UP, NMRA 1998 Convention Car, "15322", *98*	59.95	____
(00388)	Boise Cascade Wrapped Lumber Load, *98*	14.95	____
(00389)	Finlay Premium Wrapped Lumber Load, *98*	14.95	____
(00390)	Western Carrier Wrapped Lumber Load, *98*	14.95	____
(00391)	Weyerhauser Wrapped Lumber Load, *98*	14.95	____
(00392)	Pulpwood Load, *98, 02*	14.95	____
(00393)	AF Track Adaptor, 8/pkg, *00-03*	CP	____
(00394)	Bulb, 2.5-volt EVC 2/pkg, *01*	CP	____
(00395)	Rail Joiner, insulated, yel. 12/pkg, *00-02*	CP	____
(00396)	AT&SF #2 PS-2 3-bay "300142", *00, 02*	39.95	____
(00397)	Burlington Northern #2 PS-2 3-bay "435409", *00*	39.95	____
(00398)	Chessie #2 PS-2 3-bay D&O "628182", *00, 02*	39.95	____
(00399)	CB&Q #2 PS-2 3-bay "85121", *00*	39.95	____
(00400)	Chicago Northwestern #2 PS-2 3-bay "95432", *00, 02*	39.95	____
(00401)	Conrail #2 PS-2 3-bay "883672", *00, 02*	39.95	____
(00402)	GN #2 PS-2 3-bay "71971", *00*	39.95	____
(00403)	Erie Lackawanna #2 PS-2 3-bay "21892", *00, 02*	39.95	____
(00404)	New York Central #2 PS-2 3-bay "883092", *00, 02*	39.95	____
(00405)	Union Pacific #2 PS-2 3-bay "19192", *00, 02*	39.95	____
(00406)	Constant Lighting, 2.5-volt elec., *00*	CP	____
(00407)	CNW/M&StL #2 PS-2, *00, 02*	39.95	____
(00408)	LNE #2 PS-2 "18224", *00, 02*	39.95	____
(00409)	Central Soya (CSX) #2 PS-2 "145", *00, 02*	39.95	____
(00410)	Roscoe, Snyder & Pacific #2 RBLT "32", *00*	39.95	____
(00411)	Ball Lines #2 RBLT "1424", *00*	39.95	____

		Retail	Cond/S
(00412)	CB&Q (black) #1 PS-2 3-bay "85000", *00*	39.95	____
(00413)	Jack Frost #2 PS-2 "331", *00*	39.95	____
(00414)	Cedar Heights Clay PS-2 "111", *00*	39.95	____
(00415)	Ann Arbor #1 (TCA) PS-2 "781", *00*	39.95	____
(00416)	Ann Arbor #2 (TCA) PS-2 "789", *00*	39.95	____
(00417)	M&StL #1 (NASG) PS-2 3-bay "71001", *00, 02*	39.95	____
(00418)	M&StL #2 (NASG) PS-2 3-bay "71033", *00, 02*	39.95	____
(00419)	M&StL #2 (NASG) PS-2 "70525", *00, 02*	39.95	____
(00420)	CB&Q (black) #2 PS-2 3-bay "85011", *00*	39.95	____
(00421)	Conrail SW-9 set, *00*	CP	____
(00422)	BN SW-9 set, *00*	CP	____
(00423)	AT&SF SW-9 6-car set, *00*	CP	____
(00424)	Chessie SW-9 set, *00*	CP	____
(00425)	NMRA 1999 Comm. Car USRA GSV "2084", *00*	59.95	____
(00426)	Chesapeake & Ohio #1 SW-9 "5093", *00-03*	199.95	____
(00427)	Chesapeake & Ohio #2 SW-9 "5084", *00-03*	199.95	____
(00428)	Great Northern #1 SW-9 "15", *00*	199.95	____
(00429)	Great Northern #2 SW-9 "14", *00*	199.95	____
(00430)	D&RGW #1 SW-9 "133", *00-03*	199.95	____
(00431)	D&RGW #2 SW-9 "134", *00-03*	199.95	____
(00432)	ICG #1 SW-9 "1223", *00-03*	199.95	____
(00433)	ICG #2 SW-9 "1234", *00-03*	199.95	____
(00434)	Northern Pacific #1 SW-9 "133", *00-03*	199.95	____
(00435)	Northern Pacific #2 SW-9 "133", *00-03*	199.95	____
(00436)	UP (2nd sch) #1 SW-9 "1833", *00-02*	199.95	____
(00437)	UP (2nd sch) #2 SW-9 "1854", *00-02*	199.95	____
(00438)	Unlettered SW-1, *00*	CP	____
(00439)	Boston & Maine #1 SW-1 "1113", *00-02*	CP	____
(00440)	Boston & Maine #2 SW-1 "1114", *00-02*	CP	____
(00441)	Chessie System #1 SW-1 B&O "8403", *00-03*	CP	____
(00442)	Chessie System #2 SW-1 B&O "8414", *00-03*	CP	____
(00443)	C&NW #1 SW-1 "1213", *00-02*	CP	____
(00444)	C&NW #2 SW-1 "1214", *00-02*	CP	____
(00445)	WP #1 SW-1 "5103", *00-03*	CP	____
(00446)	WP #2 SW-1 "5104", *00-03*	CP	____
(00447)	Milwaukee Road #1 SW-1 "1613", *00-03*	CP	____
(00448)	Milwaukee Road #2 SW-1 "1634", *00-03*	CP	____
(00449)	PRR #1 SW-1 "5953", *00-03*	CP	____
(00450)	PRR #2 SW-1 "5944", *00-02*	CP	____
(00451)	Seaboard SW-1 "1200", *00-03*	CP	____
(00452)	Soo Line SW-1 "320", *00-03*	CP	____
(00453)	Lehigh Valley #1 SW-1, *00*	CP	____
(00454)	Lehigh Valley #2 SW-1, *00*	CP	____
(00455)	SP #1 SW-1 "1013", *00-03*	CP	____
(00456)	SP #2 SW-1 "1004", *00-03*	CP	____
(00457)	C&O SW-9 set, *00*	CP	____
(00458)	Conrail SW-9 set, *00*	CP	____
(00459)	D&RGW SW-9 set, *00*	CP	____
(00460)	GN SW-9 set, *00*	CP	____
(00461)	ICG SW-9 set, *00*	CP	____
(00462)	NP SW-9 set, *00*	CP	____
(00463)	RH No. 3 Manual Switches, *02*	CP	____

		Retail	Cond/$
(00464)	LH No. 3 Manual Switches, *02*	CP	____
(00465)	40" Flextrack (6), *02*	CP	____
(00466)	40" Flextrack (24), *02*	CP	____
(00467)	90° Crossing set, *02*	CP	____
(00468)	Bumper on 5" Straight Track (2), *02*	CP	____
(00469)	Flatcar w/ John Deere Combine, *03*	CP	____
(00470)	Flatcar w/ IH Harvestor with Combine, *03*	CP	____
(00471)	Flatcar w/ John Deere Log Skidder, *03*	CP	____
(00472)	Flatcar w/ John Deere Backhoe and Front-End Loader, *03*	CP	____
(00473)	Flatcar w/ John Deere Bulldozers, *03*	CP	____
(00474)	PRR PS-2 Two-Bay Covered Hopper, #1, *03*	CP	____
(00475)	PRR PS-2 Two-Bay Covered Hopper, #2, *03*	CP	____
(00476)	Unlettered Refrigerator Car, *00-01*	CP	____
(00477)	Unlettered yellow Refrigerator Car, *00-01*	CP	____
(00478)	Unlettered orange Refrigerator Car, *00-01*	CP	____
(00479)	ART #1 Refrigerator Car, *00*	CP	____
(00480)	ART #2 Refrigerator Car, *00*	CP	____
(00481)	AT&SF "Grande Canyon" Refrigerator Car, *01*	CP	____
(00482)	AT&SF "El Capitan" Refrigerator Car, *00*	CP	____
(00483)	BREX #1 Refrigerator Car, *01*	CP	____
(00484)	BREX #2 Refrigerator Car, *01*	CP	____
(00485)	FBX Robin Hood Beer #1 Refrigerator Car, *00*	CP	____
(00487)	GSBV Gerber #1 Refrigerator Car, *00*	CP	____
(00488)	SW Starter Boxed set, *00-01*	CP	____
(00489)	LV#1 Refrigerator Car, *01*	CP	____
(00490)	LV#2 Refrigerator Car, *01*	CP	____
(00491)	NWX gray #1 Refrigerator Car, *01-02*	CP	____
(00492)	NWX gray #2 Refrigerator Car, *01*	CP	____
(00493)	NWX green/yellow #1 Refrigerator Car, *00*	CP	____
(00494)	NWX green/yellow #2 Refrigerator Car, *00*	CP	____
(00495)	MDT #1 Refrigerator Car, *00*	CP	____
(00496)	MDT #2 Refrigerator Car, *00*	CP	____
(00497)	PGE 2000 Christmas Refrigerator Car, *00*	CP	____
(00498)	PFE #1 Refrigerator Car, *00*	CP	____
(00499)	PFE #2 Refrigerator Car, *00*	CP	____
(00500)	TUX Tivoli Beer #1 Refrigerator Car, *01-02*	CP	____
(00502)	URT A&P #1 Refrigerator Car, *00*	CP	____
(00504)	UTLX Heidelberg #1 Refrigerator Car, *00*	CP	____
(00506)	Chateau Martin #1 Refrigerator Car, *00*	CP	____
(00507)	Chateau Martin #2 Refrigerator Car, *00*	CP	____
(00508)	Chateau Martin #3 Refrigerator Car, *00*	CP	____
(00509)	CUVA #1 PS, *00*	CP	____
(00510)	CUVA #2 PS, *00*	CP	____
(00511)	Flatcar w/ John Deere excavator, *00-01*	CP	____
(00512)	Flatcar w/ asst. Bobcats, *00*	CP	____
(00513)	Berghoff Beer Refrigerator Car, *00*	CP	____
(00514)	Wilson Car Lines Refrigerator Car, *00*	CP	____
(00515)	Zion Figs Refrigerator Car, *00*	CP	____
(00516)	Ballantine Beer #1 Refrigerator Car, *00*	CP	____
(00517)	Ballantine Beer #2 Refrigerator Car, *00*	CP	____
(00518)	Parrot Potatoes Refrigerator Car, *00*	CP	____
(00519)	S Gaugian 40th Rebuilt Boxcar, *00*	CP	____

		Retail	Cond/S
(00520)	B&O 467434 Timesaver Rebuilt Boxcar, *00*	CP	____
(00521)	PRR Merchandise Service Rebuilt Boxcar, *00*	CP	____
(00522)	GN vermillion #2 Rebuilt Boxcar, *00*	CP	____
(00523)	GN vermillion #1 Rebuilt Boxcar, *00*	CP	____
(00524)	B&O 467109 Timesaver Rebuilt Boxcar, *00*	CP	____
(00525)	IGA #1 Refrigerator Car, *00*	CP	____
(00526)	IGA #2 Refrigerator Car, *00*	CP	____
(00527)	Narragansett #1 Refrigerator Car, *00*	CP	____
(00528)	Narragansett #2 Refrigerator Car, *00*	CP	____
(00529)	Flatcat w/ New Holland Grinder Mixers (3), *00*	CP	____
(00530)	Terra Gator Dry Fert SFC load, *01*	CP	____
(00531)	Terra Gator Liquid SFC load, *01*	CP	____
(00532)	Flatcar w/ John Deere Skid Loaders (4), *01*	CP	____
(00533)	TO Contr. w/ 2 wires 4+2, *01-02*	CP	____
(00534)	TO Extension 4-wire, 3/pkg., *01-02*	CP	____
(00535)	BHFC Pipe Load, *00, 02*	CP	____
(00536)	ICG Switcher 4-car set, *00*	CP	____
(00537)	Soo Switcher 5-car set, *00*	CP	____
(00538)	MILW Switcher 5-car set, *00*	CP	____
(00539)	GN Switcher 6-car set, *00*	CP	____
(00540)	Seaboard Switcher 6-car set, *00*	CP	____
(00541)	CB&Q F Unit 6-car set, *01*	CP	____
(00542)	Unlettered Double-sheathed Boxcar, *01*	CP	____
(00543)	Atlantic Coast Line Double-sheathed Boxcar, *01-02*	CP	____
(00544)	BM Line Double-sheathed Boxcar, *01-02*	CP	____
(00545)	CNW Double-sheathed Boxcar, *01-02*	CP	____
(00546)	D&LW Double-sheathed Boxcar, *01-02*	CP	____
(00547)	GN Double-sheathed Boxcar, *01-02*	CP	____
(00548)	NYC Double-sheathed Boxcar, *01-02*	CP	____
(00549)	TH&B Double-sheathed Boxcar, *01-02*	CP	____
(00550)	Union Pacific BO Double-sheathed Boxcar, *01-02*	CP	____
(00551)	IH Harvestor w/ corn load, *01*	CP	____
(00552)	Locomatic 10-button Controller, *01-02*	CP	____
(00553)	CNW SFC #1, *01-02*	CP	____
(00554)	M&StL SFC, *01-02*	CP	____
(00555)	C&NW #2 SFC, *01*	CP	____
(00556)	Conrail #1 SFC, *01-02*	CP	____
(00557)	Conrail #2 SFC, *01-02*	CP	____
(00558)	Grand Truck Western #1 SFC, *01-02*	CP	____
(00559)	Grand Truck Western #2 SFC, *01-02*	CP	____
(00560)	Reading #1 SFC, *01-02*	CP	____
(00561)	Reading #2 SFC, *01-02*	CP	____
(00562)	Union Pacific #1 SFC, *01-02*	CP	____
(00563)	Union Pacific #2 SFC, *01-02*	CP	____
(00564)	NP Christmas 2001 Double-sheathed Boxcar, *01*	CP	____
(00565)	Bulb 12.0-volt 40ma TO 2/pkg., *01-02*	CP	____
(00566)	PFE #1 orange Refrigerator Car, *01*	CP	____
(00567)	PFE #2 orange Refrigerator Car, *01*	CP	____
(00568)	LRX #1 Refrigerator Car, *01*	CP	____
(00569)	LRX #2 Refrigerator Car, *01*	CP	____
(00570)	Baby Ruth #1 Refrigerator Car, *01-02*	CP	____
(00571)	Baby Ruth #2 Refrigerator Car, *01-02*	CP	____

		Retail	Cond/S
(00572)	Ralston Refrigerator Car, *01*	CP	___
(00573)	BAR #1 Refrigerator Car, *01*	CP	___
(00574)	BAR #2 Refrigerator Car, *01*	CP	___
(00575)	MP TNO&M #1 Rebuilt, *01-02*	CP	___
(00576)	MP TNO&M #2 Rebuilt, *01-02*	CP	___
(00577)	C&NW CStP&O #1 Rebuilt, *01-02*	CP	___
(00578)	C&NW CStP&O #2 Rebuilt, *01-02*	CP	___
(00579)	CGW "C" Rebuilt, *01*	CP	___
(00580)	CGW "SL" Rebuilt, *01*	CP	___
(00581)	CGW "DF" Rebuilt, *01*	CP	___
(00582)	CGW "DFB" Rebuilt, *01*	CP	___
(00583)	Dutch Cleanser #1 Refrigerator Car, *01*	CP	___
(00584)	Land O' Lakes #1 Refrigerator Car, *01*	CP	___
(00585)	Land O' Lakes #2 Refrigerator Car, *01*	CP	___
(00586)	John Deere 430 Crawler (4) load, *01*	CP	___
(00587)	Switch Stand w/ marker light part, *01-02*	CP	___
(00588)	Coupler, F3 short-shank KD-style, *01-03*	2.95	___
(00589)	NH Skidsteers (4) load, *01-03*	CP	___
(00590)	JD Wheel Loader (1) load, *01*	CP	___
(00591)	John Deere Grader (1) load, *01*	CP	___
(00592)	Dutch Cleanser #2 Refrigerator Car, *01*	CP	___
(00593)	Chessie #3 EVC, *01-03*	69.95	___
(00594)	Chessie #4 EVC, *01-03*	69.95	___
(00595)	Chessie Safety Special EVC, *01-03*	69.95	___
(00596)	C&NW #3, *01-03*	69.95	___
(00597)	C&NW #4, *01-03*	69.95	___
(00598)	MEC (scheme II) #1 EVC, *01-03*	69.95	___
(00599)	RDG #1 EVC, *01-03*	69.95	___
(00600)	RDG #2 EVC, *01-03*	69.95	___
(00601)	Rock Island #1 EVC, *01*	69.95	___
(00602)	Rock Island #2 EVC, *01*	69.95	___
(00603)	AT&SF #4, *01-03*	69.95	___
(00604)	AT&SF #3, *01-03*	69.95	___
(00605)	CGW "C" blue Rebuilt, *01*	CP	___
(00606)	CGW "SL" blue Rebuilt, *01*	CP	___
(00607)	CGW "DF" blue Rebuilt, *01*	CP	___
(00608)	CGW "DFB" blue Rebuilt, *01*	CP	___
(00609)	CAT 609 Scraper, *01*	CP	___
(00610)	Kahn's #1 Rebuilt, *01*	CP	___
(00611)	Kahn's #2 Rebuilt, *01*	CP	___
(00612)	B&O F3 Ph2 A #1, *01*	CP	___
(00613)	B&O F3 Ph2 A #2, *01*	CP	___
(00614)	CB&Q F3 Ph2 A #1, *01*	CP	___
(00615)	CB&Q F3 Ph2 A #2, *01*	CP	___
(00616)	C&NW F3 Ph2 A #1, *01*	CP	___
(00617)	C&NW #2 F, *01*	CP	___
(00618)	DL&W F3 Ph2 A #1, *01*	CP	___
(00619)	DL&W F3 Ph2 A #2, *01*	CP	___
(00620)	MEC F3 Ph2 A #1, *01*	CP	___
(00621)	MEC F3 Ph2 A #2, *01*	CP	___
(00622)	NYC F3 Ph2 A pass #1, *01*	CP	___
(00623)	NYC F3 Ph2 A pass #2, *01*	CP	___
(00624)	Southern F3 Ph2 A #1, *01*	CP	___

		Retail	Cond/$
(00625)	Southern F3 Ph2 A #2, *01*	CP	___
(00626)	SP F3 Ph2 A #1, *01*	CP	___
(00627)	SP F3 Ph2 A #2, *01*	CP	___
(00628)	UP F3 Ph2 A #1, *01*	CP	___
(00629)	UP F3 Ph2 A #2, *01*	CP	___
(00630)	WP F3 Ph2 A #1, *01*	CP	___
(00631)	WP F3 Ph2 A #2, *01*	CP	___
(00632)	Und F3 Ph2 A, *01*	CP	___
(00633)	NYC F3 Ph2 A frt #1, *01*	CP	___
(00634)	NYC F3 Ph2 A frt #2, *01*	CP	___
(00635)	B&O F3 Ph2 B #1, *01*	CP	___
(00636)	B&O F3 Ph2 B #2, *01*	CP	___
(00637)	CB&Q F3 Ph2 B #1, *01*	CP	___
(00638)	CB&Q F3 Ph2 B #2, *01*	CP	___
(00639)	C&NW F3 Ph2 B #1, *01*	CP	___
(00640)	C&NW F3 Ph2 B #2, *01*	CP	___
(00641)	D&LW F3 Ph2 B #1, *01*	CP	___
(00642)	D&LW F3 Ph2 B #2, *01*	CP	___
(00643)	MEC F3 Ph2 B #1, *01*	CP	___
(00644)	MEC F3 Ph2 B #2, *01*	CP	___
(00645)	NYC F3 Ph2 B pass #1, *01*	CP	___
(00646)	NYC F3 Ph2 B pass #2, *01*	CP	___
(00647)	Southern F3 Ph2 B #1, *01*	CP	___
(00648)	Southern F3 Ph2 B #2, *01*	CP	___
(00649)	SP F3 Ph2 B #1, *01*	CP	___
(00650)	SP F3 Ph2 B #2, *01*	CP	___
(00651)	UP F3 Ph2 B #1, *01*	CP	___
(00652)	UP F3 Ph2 B #2, *01*	CP	___
(00653)	WP F3 Ph2 B #1, *01*	CP	___
(00654)	WP F3 Ph2 B #2, *01*	CP	___
(00655)	Und F3 Ph2 B, *01*	CP	___
(00656)	NYC F3 Ph2 B frt #1, *01*	CP	___
(00657)	NYC F3 Ph2 B frt #2 B239, *01*	CP	___
(00658)	Brookside Milk Refrigerator Car, *03*	CP	___
(00659)	Saval BAF "003A" Refrigerator Car, *03*	CP	___
(00660)	Metal Rail Joiners (36) Track, *01*	CP	___
(00661)	PRR MS Xm Rebuilt, *01-02*	CP	___
(00662)	GN orange/green #1 Rebuilt, *01-02*	CP	___
(00663)	GN orange/green #1 Rebuilt, *01-02*	CP	___
(00664)	33" wheels Caboose 4/set parts, *01*	CP	___
(00665)	Speaker, 36 mm-dia parts, *01*	CP	___
(00666)	Chessie Switcher 6-car set, *01-02*	CP	___
(00667)	MU Cables (pair) parts, *01*	CP	___
(00668)	Gearbox code 110, *01*	CP	___
(00669)	Gearbox code AF-comp., *01*	CP	___
(00670)	5" Induction Coil (uncoupler) Track, *02-03*	CP	___
(00671)	5" Third Rail (accessory track), *01*	CP	___
(00672)	CAT D6R XL Bulldozer (2) loads, *01-02*	CP	___
(00673)	CAT D25D Art. Truck loads, *01-02*	CP	___
(00674)	CAT 950F Wheel Loader loads, *01-02*	CP	___
(00675)	CAT 12G Grader loads, *01-02*	CP	___
(00676)	CAT Challenger Tractor (2) loads, *01-02*	CP	___
(00677)	CAT Boom Sprayer set loads, *01-02*	CP	___

		Retail	Cond/$
(00678)	CAT Simonsen Spreader set loads, *01-02*	CP	____
(00679)	CAT Knight Slinger set loads, *01-02*	CP	____
(00680)	CAT D6R Bulldozer (2) loads, *01-02*	CP	____
(00681)	CAT 611 Scraper loads, *01*	CP	____
(00682)	PFE orange #1 Refrigerator Car, 3-car set, *01-02*	CP	____
(00683)	BREX #1 Refrigerator Car, 3-car set, *01-02*	CP	____
(00684)	NWX yellow/green #1 Refrigerator Car, 3-car set, *01-02*	CP	____
(00685)	ART #1 Refrigerator Car, 3-car set, *01*	CP	____
(00686)	NP #1 Refrigerator Car, *01-02*	CP	____
(00687)	NP #2 Refrigerator Car, *01*	CP	____
(00688)	AT&SF (JH) Rebuilt, *01*	CP	____
(00689)	Boston & Maine (JH) Rebuilt, *01*	CP	____
(00690)	Rio Grande white Rebuilt, *01*	CP	____
(00691)	Rio Grande aluminum Rebuilt, *01*	CP	____
(00692)	C&NW SW 5-car set, *01*	CP	____
(00693)	C&NW F 6-car set, *01-02*	CP	____
(00694)	MEC F 5-car set, *01-02*	CP	____
(00695)	FGE #1 Refrigerator Car, 3-car set, *01-02*	CP	____
(00697)	Edelweiss Beer 40' Wood Refrigerator Car, *02*	CP	____
(00698)	Kraft Cheese 40' Wood Refrigerator Car, *02*	CP	____
(00699)	CN 40' Wood Refrigerator Car, *02*	CP	____
(00700)	CN 40' Wood Refrigerator Car, *02*	CP	____
(00701)	B&M 40' Rebuilt Boxcar, 1, *03*	CP	____
(00702)	B&M 40' Rebuilt Boxcar, 2, *03*	CP	____
(00703)	Santa Fe "Shock Control" 40' Rebuilt Boxcar 1, *03*	CP	____
(00704)	Santa Fe "Shock Control" 40' Rebuilt Boxcar 2, *03*	CP	____
(00706)	D&RGW "Cookie Box" 40' Rebuilt Boxcar (white), 2, *03*	CP	____
(00707)	D&RGW "Cookie Box" 40' Rebuilt Boxcar (Silver), 1, *03*	CP	____
(00708)	D&RGW "Cookie Box" 40' Rebuilt Boxcar (Silver), 2, *03*	CP	____
(00709)	Central of Georgia 40' Rebuilt Boxcar, 1, *03*	CP	____
(00709)	CB&Q F3A Diesel 6-car Freight set, *03*	CP	____
(00710)	Central of Georgia 40' Rebuilt Boxcar, 2", *03*	CP	____
(00713)	NP SW9 Diesel 4-car Freight set, *03*	CP	____
(00714)	Milwaukee Road SW1 Diesel 5-car Freight set, *02*	CP	____
(00715)	CB&Q F3 Diesel 6-car Freight set, *02*	CP	____
(00716)	Santa Fe 40' Wood Refrigerator Car, *02*	CP	____
(00717)	Undec. 40' Wood Refrigerator Car, red, *02*	CP	____
(00720)	Saval BAF "00313" Refrigerator Car, *03*	CP	____
(00721)	B&O 40' Steel Rebuilt Boxcar "467448", *02*	CP	____
(00722)	B&O 40' Steel Rebuilt Boxcar "467153", *02*	CP	____
(00723)	Undecorated Ore Car, black, *02*	CP	____
(00724)	Undecorated Ore Car, red, *02*	CP	____
(00725)	DM&IR Ore Car, *02*	CP	____
(00726)	DM&IR Ore Car 3-pack, *02*	CP	____
(00727)	B&LE Ore Car, *02*	CP	____
(00728)	B&LE Ore Car 3-pack, *02*	CP	____
(00729)	CN Ore Car, *02*	CP	____

		Retail	Cond/$
(00730)	CN Ore Car 3-pack, *02*	CP	____
(00731)	CP Ore Car, *02*	CP	____
(00732)	CP Ore Car 3-pack, *02*	CP	____
(00733)	C&NWR Ore Car, *02-03*	CP	____
(00734)	C&NW Ore Car 3-pack, *02-03*	CP	____
(00735)	GN Ore Car, *02-03*	CP	____
(00736)	GN Ore Car 3-pack, *02-03*	CP	____
(00737)	Milwaukee Road Ore Car, *02-03*	CP	____
(00738)	Milwaukee Road Ore Car 3-pack, *02-03*	CP	____
(00739)	Soo Line Ore Car, *02-03*	CP	____
(00740)	Soo Line Ore Car 3-pack, *02-03*	CP	____
(00741)	SP Ore Car, *02-03*	CP	____
(00742)	SP Ore Car 3-pack, *02-03*	CP	____
(00743)	UP Ore Car, *02-03*	CP	____
(00744)	UP Ore Car 3-pack, *02-03*	CP	____
(00745)	DCC SoundTrax Sound Decoder, *02-03*	160	____
(00746)	Santa Fe 40' Steel Rebuilt Boxcar "14893", *02-03*	CP	____
(00747)	C&NW 40' Steel Rebuilt Boxcar "65262", *02-03*	CP	____
(00748)	NYC (P&LE) 40' Steel Rebuilt Boxcar "36203", *02-03*	CP	____
(00749)	UP 40' Steel Rebuilt Boxcar "20442", *02-03*	CP	____
(00752)	NYC (Michigan Central) 40' Single-Sheathed Wood Boxcar "80912", *02-03*	CP	____
(00755)	C&NW 40' Stockcar "14793", *02-03*	CP	____
(00756)	NYC (CCC&StL) 40' Stockcar "20442", *02-03*	CP	____
(00757)	UP 40' Stockcar "48216", *02-03*	CP	____
(00760)	Ann Arbor 55-Ton Twin Hopper Car 3-pack, *02-03*	CP	____
(00761)	Ann Arbor 55-Ton Twin Hopper Car, *02-03*	CP	____
(00762)	Santa Fe 55-Ton Twin Hopper Car 3-pack, *02-03*	CP	____
(00763)	Santa Fe 55-Ton Twin Hopper Car, *02-03*	CP	____
(00764)	B&O 55-Ton Twin Hopper Car 3-pack, *02-03*	CP	____
(00765)	B&O 55-Ton Twin Hopper Car, *02-03*	CP	____
(00766)	C&O 55-Ton Twin Hopper Car 3-pack, *02-03*	CP	____
(00767)	C&O 55-Ton Twin Hopper Car, *02-03*	CP	____
(00768)	CB&Q 55-Ton Twin Hopper Car 3-pack, *02-03*	CP	____
(00769)	CB&Q 55-Ton Twin Hopper Car, *02-03*	CP	____
(00770)	LV 55-Ton Twin Hopper Car 3-pack, *02-03*	CP	____
(00771)	LV 55-Ton Twin Hopper Car, *02-03*	CP	____
(00773)	Clinchfield 55-Ton Twin Hopper Car, *03*	CP	____
(00776)	NKP 55-Ton Twin Hopper Car 3-pack, *02-03*	CP	____
(00777)	NKP 55-Ton Twin Hopper Car, *02-03*	CP	____
(00780)	Virginian 55-Ton Twin Hopper Car 3-pack, *02-03*	CP	____
(00781)	Virginian 55-Ton Twin Hopper Car, *02-03*	CP	____
(00782)	Wabash 55-Ton Twin Hopper Car 3-pack, *02-03*	CP	____
(00783)	Wabash 55-Ton Twin Hopper Car, *02-03*	CP	____
(00784)	RH No. 6 Remote Control Switches, *02-03*	CP	____
(00785)	LH No. 6 Remote Control Switches, *02-03*	CP	____
(00786)	RH No. 6 Manual Switches, *02-03*	CP	____
(00787)	LH No. 6 Manual Switches, *02-03*	CP	____
(00788)	Feeder Wire Terminal (24), *02-03*	CP	____
(00789)	DCC F3 Wire Harness, *02-03*	CP	____
(00790)	DCC F3 Wire Harness, *02-03*	CP	____
(00791)	DCC Sound Manual, *02-03*	CP	____

		Retail	Cond/$
(00792)	RH No. 5 Remote Control Switches, *02-03*	CP	_____
(00793)	LH No. 5 Remote Control Switches, *02-03*	CP	_____
(00794)	RH No. 5 Manual Switches, *02-03*	CP	_____
(00796)	LH No. 5 Manual Switches, *02-03*	CP	_____
(00801)	Borden's 40' Billboard Refrigerator Car, *03*	CP	_____
(00804)	Swift 40' Billboard Refrigerator Car 3-pack, *03*	CP	_____
(00808)	Frisco 40' Boxcar 3-pack, *03*	CP	_____
(00810)	Santa Fe EMD F7 Passenger A Unit "206", *03*	CP	_____
(00811)	Santa Fe EMD F7 Freight A Unit "206L", *03*	CP	_____
(00814)	B&M EMD F7 A Unit "4265", *03*	CP	_____
(00816)	D&RGW EMD F7 A Unit "5554", *03*	CP	_____
(00818)	GN EMD F7 A Unit "454-D", *03*	CP	_____
(00820)	MP EMD F7 A Unit "587", *03*	CP	_____
(00822)	Pennsylvania EMD F7 A Unit "3654", *03*	CP	_____
(00825)	Santa Fe EMD F7 Passenger B Unit, *03*	CP	_____
(00826)	Santa Fe EMD F7 Freight B Unit, *03*	CP	_____
(00829)	B&M EMD F7 B Unit, *03*	CP	_____
(00831)	D&RGW EMD F7 B Unit, *03*	CP	_____
(00833)	GN EMD F7 B Unit, *03*	CP	_____
(00835)	MP EMD F7 B Unit, *03*	CP	_____
(00837)	Pennsylvania EMD F7 B Unit, *03*	CP	_____
(00923)	Kahn's 40' Billboard Refrigerator Car, #1, *03*	CP	_____
(00924)	Kahn's 40' Billboard Refrigerator Car, #2, *03*	CP	_____
(00925)	Control Button, *03*	CP	_____
(00926)	Unlighted 5" Bumper, *03*	CP	_____
(00966)	CNJ PS-2 Two-Bay Covered Hopper, *03*	40	_____
(00972)	Jack Frost PS-2 Three-Bay Covered Hopper, *03*	CP	_____
(00973)	G&W PS-2 Three-Bay Covered Hopper, #1, *03*	CP	_____
(00974)	G&W PS-2 Three-Bay Covered Hopper, #2, *03*	CP	_____
(00975)	Reading PS-2 Three-Bay Covered Hopper, #1, *03*	CP	_____
(00976)	Reading PS-2 Three-Bay Covered Hopper, #2, *03*	CP	_____
(00977)	Wabash PS-2 Three-Bay Covered Hopper, #1, *03*	CP	_____
(00978)	Wabash PS-2 Three-Bay Covered Hopper, #2, *03*	CP	_____
(00980)	Unlet. Side-Panel Hopper, Black, *03*	CP	_____
(00981)	Unlet. Side-Panel Hopper, Red, *03*	CP	_____
(00982)	Anderson Side-Panel Hopper, #1, 3-pack, *03*	CP	_____
(00983)	Anderson Side-Panel Hopper, #4, *03*	CP	_____
(00984)	Ann Arbor Side-Panel Hopper, #1, 3-pack, *03*	CP	_____
(00985)	Ann Arbor Side-Panel Hopper, #4, *03*	CP	_____
(00986)	C&O Side-Panel Hopper, #1, 3-pack, *03*	CP	_____
(00987)	C&O Side-Panel Hopper, #4, *03*	CP	_____
(00988)	Frisco Side-Panel Hopper, #1, 3-pack, *03*	CP	_____
(00989)	Frisco Side-Panel Hopper, #4, *03*	CP	_____
(00990)	D&H Side-Panel Hopper, #1, 3-pack, *03*	CP	_____
(00991)	D&H Side-Panel Hopper, #4, *03*	CP	_____
(00994)	NYC Side-Panel Hopper, #1, 3-pack, *03*	CP	_____
(00995)	NYC Side-Panel Hopper, #4, *03*	CP	_____
(00996)	NH Side-Panel Hopper, #1, *03*	CP	_____
(00997)	Pennsylvania Side-Panel Hopper, #1, *03*	CP	_____
(00998)	Wabash Side-Panel Hopper, #1, 3-pack, *03*	CP	_____
(00999)	Wabash Side-Panel Hopper, #4, *03*	CP	_____
(01000)	PFE 40' Billboard Refrigerator Car, #1, *03*	CP	_____
(01001)	PFE 40' Billboard Refrigerator Car, #2, *03*	CP	_____

		Retail	Cond/$
(01002)	ART/MP 40' Billboard Refrigerator Car, #1, *03*	CP	____
(01003)	ART/MP 40' Billboard Refrigerator Car, #2, *03*	CP	____
(01006)	Northern Refrigerator Banana Car 40' Billboard Refrigerator Car, *03*	CP	____
(01007)	Schlitz Beer 40' Billboard Refrigerator Car, *03*	CP	____
(01008)	MP 40' Steel "Rebuilt" Boxcar, #1, *03*	CP	____
(01009)	MP 40' Steel "Rebuilt" Boxcar, #2, *03*	CP	____
(01010)	CN 40' Steel "Rebuilt" Boxcar, #1, *03*	CP	____
(01011)	CN 40' Steel "Rebuilt" Boxcar, #2, *03*	CP	____
(01012)	Seaboard 40' Steel "Rebuilt" Boxcar, Orange Blossom Special, *03*	CP	____
(01013)	Seaboard 40' Steel "Rebuilt" Boxcar, Silver Meteor, *03*	CP	____
(01014)	Santa Fe 40' Steel "Rebuilt" Boxcar, Super Chief, *03*	CP	____
(01016)	FGEX 40' Billboard Refrigerator Car, #1, *03*	CP	____
(01017)	Century Beer 40' Billboard Refrigerator Car, *03*	CP	____
(01018)	Burlington Route 40' Rebuilt Boxcar, #1, *03*	CP	____
(01016)	FGEX 40' Billboard Refrigerator Car, #2, *03*	CP	____
(01019)	Burlington Route 40' Rebuilt Boxcar, #2, *03*	CP	____
(01020)	State of Maine BAR 40' Rebuilt Boxcar, *03*	CP	____
(01021)	State of Maine NH 40' Rebuilt Boxcar, *03*	CP	____
(01022)	L&N "Dixie" 40' Rebuilt Boxcar, #1, *03*	CP	____
(01023)	L&N "Dixie" 40' Rebuilt Boxcar, #2, *03*	CP	____
(01024)	WP 40' Rebuilt Boxcar, #1, *03*	CP	____
(01025)	WP 40' Rebuilt Boxcar, #2, *03*	CP	____
(01026)	PRR/DF 40' Rebuilt Boxcar, #1, *03*	CP	____
(01027)	PRR/DF 40' Rebuilt Boxcar, #2, *03*	CP	____
(01028)	NYC Pacemaker 40' Rebuilt Boxcar, #1, *03*	CP	____
(01029)	NYC Pacemaker 40' Rebuilt Boxcar, #2, *03*	CP	____
(01030)	NYC Pacemaker 40' Rebuilt Boxcar, #3, *03*	CP	____
(01032)	Tipo Wine Refrigerator Car, #1, *03*	CP	____
(01033)	Tipo Wine Refrigerator Car, #2, *03*	CP	____
(01034)	Santa Fe F7 Diesel 6-car Freight set, *03*	CP	____
(01036)	MP F7 Diesel 6-car Freight set, *03*	CP	____
(01037)	S-Trax Bumper 2-pack, *03*	CP	____
(01038)	S-Trax Bumper 2-pack, *03*	CP	____
(01043)	ICG SW9 Diesel 4-car Freight set, *03*	CP	____
(01044)	Rio Grande SW9 Diesel 5-car Freight set, *03*	CP	____
(01046)	MEC F3 Diesel 5-car Freight set, *03*	CP	____
(01045)	Seaboard SWII Diesel 5-car Freight set, *03*	CP	____
(01049)	GTW Side-Panel Hopper, #4, *03*	CP	____
(01050)	GTW Side-Panel Hopper, #1, 3-pack, *03*	CP	____
(01052)	B&O 2-8-0 Steam Locomotive #1, AC/DC, *03*	CP	____
(01053)	B&O 2-8-0 Steam Locomotive #2, AC/DC, *03*	CP	____
(01054)	Santa Fe 2-8-0 Steam Locomotive #1, AC/DC, *03*	CP	____
(01056)	C&NW 2-8-0 Steam Locomotive #1, AC/DC, *03*	CP	____
(01058)	Erie 2-8-0 Steam Locomotive #1, AC/DC, *03*	CP	____
(01059)	Erie 2-8-0 Steam Locomotive #2, AC/DC, *03*	CP	____
(01060)	MEC 2-8-0 Steam Locomotive #1, AC/DC, *03*	CP	____
(01061)	MEC 2-8-0 Steam Locomotive #2, AC/DC, *03*	CP	____
(01062)	NYC 2-8-0 Steam Locomotive #1, AC/DC, *03*	CP	____
(01063)	NYC 2-8-0 Steam Locomotive #2, AC/DC, *03*	CP	____

		Retail	Cond/S
(01064)	Southern 2-8-0 Steam Locomotive #1, AC/DC, *03*	CP	____
(01066)	Southern 2-8-0 Steam Locomotive #2, AC/DC, *03*	CP	____
(01066)	UP 2-8-0 Steam Locomotive #1, AC/DC, *03*	CP	____
(01067)	UP 2-8-0 Steam Locomotive #2, AC/DC, *03*	CP	____
(01068)	WM 2-8-0 Steam Locomotive #1, AC/DC, *03*	CP	____
(01069)	WM 2-8-0 Steam Locomotive #2, AC/DC, *03*	CP	____
(01070)	Flatcar w/ Oliver Corn Picker, *03*	CP	____
(01071)	Unlet. 2-8-0 Steam Locomotive #1, AC/DC, *03*	CP	____
(01072)	B&O 2-8-0 Steam Locomotive #1, DCC Sound, *03*	CP	____
(01073)	B&O 2-8-0 Steam Locomotive #2, DCC Sound, *03*	CP	____
(01074)	Santa Fe 2-8-0 Steam Locomotive #1, DCC Sound, *03*	CP	____
(01075)	Santa Fe 2-8-0 Steam Locomotive #2, DCC Sound, *03*	CP	____
(01076)	C&NW 2-8-0 Steam Locomotive #1, DCC Sound, *03*	CP	____
(01077)	C&NW 2-8-0 Steam Locomotive #2, DCC Sound, *03*	CP	____
(01078)	Erie 2-8-0 Steam Locomotive #1, DCC Sound, *03*	CP	____
(01079)	Erie 2-8-0 Steam Locomotive #2, DCC Sound, *03*	CP	____
(01080)	MEC 2-8-0 Steam Locomotive #1, DCC Sound, *03*	CP	____
(01081)	MEC 2-8-0 Steam Locomotive #2, DCC Sound, *03*	CP	____
(01082)	NYC 2-8-0 Steam Locomotive #1, DCC Sound, *03*	CP	____
(01083)	NYC 2-8-0 Steam Locomotive #2, DCC Sound, *03*	CP	____
(01084)	Southern 2-8-0 Steam Locomotive #1, DCC Sound, *03*	CP	____
(01086)	Southern 2-8-0 Steam Locomotive #2, DCC Sound, *03*	CP	____
(01086)	UP 2-8-0 Steam Locomotive #1, DCC Sound, *03*	CP	____
(01087)	UP 2-8-0 Steam Locomotive #2, DCC Sound, *03*	CP	____
(01088)	WM 2-8-0 Steam Locomotive #1, DCC Sound, *03*	CP	____
(01089)	WM 2-8-0 Steam Locomotive #2, DCC Sound, *03*	CP	____
(01090)	Flatcar w/ IH Farmall Corn Picker, *03*	CP	____
(01091)	Unlet. 2-8-0 Steam Locomotive #2, DCC Sound, *03*	CP	____
(01092)	B&O 2-8-0 Steam Locomotive #1, DCC, *03*	CP	____
(01093)	B&O 2-8-0 Steam Locomotive #2, DCC, *03*	CP	____
(01094)	Santa Fe 2-8-0 Steam Locomotive #1, DCC, *03*	CP	____
(01095)	Santa Fe 2-8-0 Steam Locomotive #2, DCC, *03*	CP	____
(01096)	C&NW 2-8-0 Steam Locomotive #1, DCC, *03*	CP	____
(01097)	C&NW 2-8-0 Steam Locomotive #2, DCC, *03*	CP	____
(01098)	Erie 2-8-0 Steam Locomotive #1, DCC, *03*	CP	____
(01099)	Erie 2-8-0 Steam Locomotive #2, DCC, *03*	CP	____
(01100)	MEC 2-8-0 Steam Locomotive #1, DCC, *03*	CP	____
(01101)	MEC 2-8-0 Steam Locomotive #2, DCC, *03*	CP	____
(01102)	NYC 2-8-0 Steam Locomotive #1, DCC, *03*	CP	____
(01103)	NYC 2-8-0 Steam Locomotive #2, DCC, *03*	CP	____
(01104)	Southern 2-8-0 Steam Locomotive #2, DCC, *03*	CP	____
(01105)	Southern 2-8-0 Steam Locomotive #1, DCC, *03*	CP	____
(01106)	UP 2-8-0 Steam Locomotive #1, DCC, *03*	CP	____
(01107)	UP 2-8-0 Steam Locomotive #2, DCC, *03*	CP	____
(01108)	WM 2-8-0 Steam Locomotive #1, DCC, *03*	CP	____
(01109)	WM 2-8-0 Steam Locomotive #2, DCC, *03*	CP	____
(01111)	Unlet. 2-8-0 Steam Locomotive #2, DCC, *03*	CP	____

		Retail	Cond/$
(01210)	Flatcar w/ Case IH Grinder Mixers, *03*	CP	____
(01213)	Flatcar w/ John Deere Corn Picker, *03*	CP	____
(01214)	RH No. 6 Code 110 Switch, *03*	CP	____
(01215)	LH No. 6 Code 110 Switch, *03*	CP	____
(01216)	RH No. 8 Code 110 Switch, *03*	CP	____
(01217)	LH No. 8 Code 110 Switch, *03*	CP	____
(01218)	40" Flextrack Code 110, *03*	CP	____
(01219)	Homabed Straight, *03*	CP	____
(01220)	Homabed Curve, *03*	CP	____
(01221)	Homabed straight/curve, *03*	CP	____
(01222)	Monon 55-Ton Twin Hopper Car 3-pack, *03*	CP	____
(01223)	Monon 55-Ton Twin Hopper Car, *03*	CP	____
(01224)	LV 55-Ton Twin Hopper Car 3-pack, *03*	CP	____
(01226)	LV 55-Ton Twin Hopper Car, *03*	CP	____
(01226)	PRR 55-Ton Twin Hopper Car 3-pack, *03*	CP	____
(01227)	Pennsylvania 55-Ton Twin Hopper Car, *03*	CP	____
(ART-5400)	DC Power Pack, 24VDC, *02-03*	50	____
(KID-802)	Kadee 802 Coupler w/ Screws (2), *02-03*	3	____
(TC100)	Scale Track Cleaning Car, *03*	CP	____
(TC101)	AF-Compatible Track Cleaning Car, *03*	CP	____
No Number	Train Pack Lube set, *02-03*	15	____

GILBERT PAPER
1946–1966

		Good	Exc	Cond/$
1946				
D1451	Consumer Catalog, *46*			
	(A) As above	35	125	____
	(B) w/ red binder	75	395	____
No number	Envelope for D1451, *46*	2.50	7	____
D1455	Dealer Catalog, *46*	27	100	____
D1457	Gilbert Scientific Toys, *46*	10	21	____
D1458	Appointment Card, *46*	0.50	1.50	____
M2499	Instruction Sheet, *46*	0.25	0.90	____
1947				
D1462	Catalog Mailer, *47*	14	60	____
D1472	Catalog Mailer, *47*	14	60	____
D1473	Consumer Catalog, *47*	27	90	____
No number	Envelope for D1473, *47*	2.50	4	____
D1482	Dealer Catalog, *47*	20	50	____
D1492	Erector Fun and Action, *47*	4	13	____
D1495	What Retail Stores Should Know, *47*	4	13	____
D1496	Display Suggestions, *47*	45	270	____
D1502	Advance Catalog, *47*	13	41	____
M2502	Instruction Book, *47*	2	4	____
1948				
D1505	Advance Catalog, *48*	10	38	____
D1507	Consumer Catalog, *48*	15	75	____
D1508	Superman, *48*	15	70	____
D1508	Consumer Catalog, *48*			
	(A) As above	10	27	____
	(B) Postage Prepaid	5	18	____
D1517	HO Catalog, *48*	9	23	____
1949				
D1524	Gilbert Scientific Toys Catalog, *49*	5	9	____
D1525	Bang Bang Torpedo, *49*	45	90	____
D1530	Advance Catalog, *49*	18	41	____
D1531	Gilbert Scientific Toys Catalog, *49*	5	9	____
D1535	Consumer Catalog, *49*		NRS	____
D1536	Consumer Catalog, *49*	9	43	____
D1547	Catalog Envelope, *49*	1.50	4	____
D1552	How to Sell American Flyer, *49*	5	18	____
M2690	Instruction Booklet, *49*			
	(A) Yellow cover	1.50	5	____
	(B) White cover	4	10	____
1950				
D1578	Dealer Catalog, *50*	13	60	____
D1579	Gilbert Toys, *50*	5	16	____
D1581/D1581A	Red/blue Ad, *50*		NRS	____
D1604	Consumer Catalog, *50*	16	60	____
D1610	Catalog Envelope, *50*	1.50	4	____
D1629	Dealer Action Displays Sheet, *50*		NRS	____

		Good	Exc	Cond/S
D1631	Dealer TV Ad, *50*	9	18	____
No number Ready Again Booklet, *50*			300	____

1951

		Good	Exc	Cond/S
D1637	Dealer Catalog, *51*	11	30	____
D1637A	Advance Catalog, *51*	8	25	____
D1640	Consumer Catalog, *51*	15	49	____
D1641	Erector and Gilbert Toys Catalog, *51*	2.50	5	____
D1652	Facts About AF Trains, *51*		NRS	____
D1656	AF and Toys, *51*	5	9	____
D1660	Gilbert Electric Eye, *51*	5	9	____

1952

		Good	Exc	Cond/S
D1667	Advance Catalog, *52*	10	41	____
D1667A	Advance Catalog, *52*	11	35	____
D1668A	Consumer Catalog, *52*		65	____
D1670	Single Sheet 200 Series Bldgs., *52*	2.50	9	____
D1677	Consumer Catalog, *52*	8	34	____
D1678	Facts About AF Trains, *52*	7	11	____
M2978	AF Model Railroad Handbook, *52*	5	10	____
M2984	Instruction Book, *52*	1	4	____
No number Advance Catalog, *52*			NRS	____
No Number Consumer Catalog, Spanish, *52*			NRS	____

1953

		Good	Exc	Cond/S
D1699	Consumer Catalog, *53*		NRS	____
D1703	Erector and Other Toys, *53*	3	7	____
D1704	Dealer Catalog, *53*	9	38	____
D1714	Dealer Catalog, East, *53*	8	23	____
D1715	Consumer Catalog, West, *53*	11	33	____
D1727	Tips on Selling AF Trains, *53*	5	9	____
D1728	Tips on Erector, *53*	2.50	8	____

1954

		Good	Exc	Cond/S
D1734	Catalog Envelope, *54*	1.50	4	____
D1740	Erector and Gilbert Toys, *54*	0.85	4	____
D1744	AF and Erector Ad Program, *54*	4	16	____
D1746	Dealer Catalog, *54*			
	(A) Pulp	8	22	____
	(B) Glossy	8	26	____
D1748	Catalog, East, *54*			
	(A) Consumer	3	13	____
	(B) Dealer	4	16	____
D1749	Dealer Catalog, West, *54*	11	27	____
D1750	Dealer Displays, *54*		NRS	____
D1751	Microscope Flysheet, *54*	0.85	2.50	____
D1760	Consumer Catalog, East, *54*	10	35	____
D1761	Consumer Catalog, West, *54*	12	36	____
D1762	Boys RR Club Letter, *54*	1.50	4	____
D1769	Read All About Ad Campaign, *54*		NRS	____
D1774	Erector and Other Gilbert Toys, *54*	2.50	5	____
D1777	Reply Postcard, *54*	0.85	2.50	____
M3290	Instruction Book, *54*	1.50	4	____

1955

		Good	Exc	Cond/S
D1782	Dealer Catalog, *55*	8	27	____
D1783	Certificate of Registry, *55*	5	9	____
D1784	Erector and Other Gilbert Toys, *55*		80	____
D1801	Consumer Catalog, East, *55*	7	27	____
D1802	Consumer Catalog, West, *55*	9	23	____
D1814	Choo Choo Sound Foldout, *55*	0.85	4	____
D1816	Dealer Catalog, *55*	9	22	____
D1820	HO Consumer Catalog, *55*	0.95	3	____
D1835	Tips for Selling Erector, *55*	0.85	2.50	____
D1840	Envelope, *55*	0.85	4	____
M3450	Instruction Book, *55*	1	4	____

1956

		Good	Exc	Cond/S
D1866	Consumer Catalog, East, *56*	7	33	____
D1867	Consumer Catalog, West, *56*	10	30	____
D1874	Dealer Catalog, *56*	14	37	____
D1879	Gilbert and Erector Toys, *56*	0.90	6	____
D1882	AF and Erector Displays, *56*	0.90	6	____
D1899	Big Value American Flyer Railroad Trestle System Special Set Brochure, *56*		100	____
D1904	Gilbert HO Catalog, *56*	2	11	____
D1907	Dealer Catalog, *56*	6	25	____
D1920	How to Build a Model Railroad, *56*	2	9	____
D1922	Miniature Catalog, *56*	6	25	____
D1925	Erector Folder, *56*	2	7	____
D1926	Envelope for D1922 Catalog, *56*	1.50	4	____

1957

		Good	Exc	Cond/S
D1937	Dealer Catalog, *57*	9	19	____
D1966	Consumer Catalog, *57*	2	7	____
D1973	Erector and Other Toys, *57*	0.85	2.50	____
D1980	Cardboard, *57*		35	____
D1981	Same as D1980, *57*		35	____
D2006	Consumer Catalog, East, *57*	5	26	____
D2007	Consumer Catalog, West, *57*	13	40	____
D2008	Erector and Toys, *57*	0.85	4	____
D2022	Dealer Flyer, *57*		50	____
D2031	Consumer Catalog, *57*		50	____
D2037	Erector and Gilbert Toys, *57*	0.85	5	____
D2045	Gilbert Promotion Kit, *57*		NRS	____
M3817	HO Instructions, *57*	2	7	____
No number	Same as M3450 (1955) but w/o number, *57*		20	____

1958

		Good	Exc	Cond/S
D2047	Consumer Catalog, *58*	21	90	____
D2048	Catalog, West, *58*	25	70	____
D2058	Erector and Toys, *58*	0.85	4	____
D2060	Erector and Gilbert Toys, *58*	2	9	____

		Good	Exc	Cond/$
D2073	Advance Catalog, *58*	6	17	_____
D2080	Smoking Caboose, *58*		125	_____
D2086	Consumer Folder, East, *58*	2.50	13	_____
D2087	Consumer Folder, West, *58*	1	11	_____
D2088	Consumer Folder, *58*	2.50	13	_____
D2101	Career Building Science Toys, *58*	0.85	2.50	_____
D4106	HO Catalog, *58*	1.50	5	_____
M4195	Accessory Folder, *58*	0.85	4	_____
M4202	Color Billboards, *58*		NRS	_____

1959

		Good	Exc	Cond/$
D2115	Dealer Catalog, *59*	12	34	_____
No Number Canadian, D2115, *59*			NRS	_____
D2118	AF No. 20142, Willit, *59*		15	_____
D2120	Career Building Science Toys, *59*	0.85	4	_____
D2125	Overland Express Sheet, *59*	0.85	2.50	_____
D2146	Consumer Catalog, *59*	1	9	_____
D2148	Consumer Catalog, *59*	0.95	6	_____
D2171-D2179 Dealer Promotional Set, *59*			NRS	_____
D2179	Promotional Sheet, Franklin Set, *59*	0.95	5	_____
D2180	Gilbert Science Toys, *59*	0.85	4	_____
No Number Catalog, Gilbert toys, *59*			NRS	_____
M4225	Train Assembly and Operating Instructions, *59*		NRS	_____
M4326	Accessory Catalog, *59*	0.85	4	_____
M4869	AF Maintenance Manual, *59*	0.85	2.50	_____

1960

		Good	Exc	Cond/$
D2192	Catalog, *60*			
	(A) Dealer	5	13	_____
	(B) Advance		30	_____
D2193	Consumer Catalog, *60*	2	9	_____
D2193REV Revised Consumer Catalog, *60*		2	7	_____
D2198	Action and Fun Catalog, *60*	2.50	6	_____
D2205	Gilbert Toys, *60*	2	4	_____
D2208	Dealer Advance Catalog, *60*		75	_____
D2223	Gilbert Science Toys, *60*	1	4	_____
D2224	Consumer Folder, *60*	1.50	5	_____
D2225	Consumer Folder, *60*	3	6	_____
D2226	Consumer Folder, *60*	1.50	4	_____
D2230	Consumer Catalog, *60*	9	40	_____
D2231	Consumer Catalog, *60*	2.50	9	_____
No Number Promotional Sheet, Truscott Set, *60*		50	_____

1961

		Good	Exc	Cond/$
D2238	Career Building Science Toys, *61*	2.50	13	_____
D2239	Consumer Catalog, *61*	4	19	_____
D2242REV Auto Rama Catalog, *61*		0.55	2.50	_____
D2255	1961-62 Retail Display, *61*	0.50	2	_____
D2266	Gilbert Science Toys, *61*	1	6	_____
D2267	Consumer Catalog, *61*	4	15	_____
D2268	Auto Rama Folder, *61*	0.50	2	_____

1962

		Good	Exc	Cond/$
No number	The Big Ones Come From Gilbert, *62*		35	____
D2277REV	Career Building Science Toys, *62*	7	23	____
D2278	Dealer Catalog, *62*	2.50	15	____
D2278REV	Revised Dealer Catalog, *62*	2	10	____
D2282	Dealer Catalog, *62*		35	____
D2283	HO Trains and Accessories, *62*	2	7	____
D2307	Consumer Ad Mats, *62*		75	____
D2310	Consumer Catalog, *62*	4	17	____
M6874	Instruction Booklet, *62*	0.85	4	____

1963

		Good	Exc	Cond/$
D2321	Dealer Catalog, *63*	1.50	4	____
D2321REV	Revised Dealer Catalog, *63*	5	16	____
D2328	Consumer Catalog, *63*		30	____
X863-3	Consumer Catalog, *63*	4	16	____

1964

		Good	Exc	Cond/$
X-264-6	Consumer Catalog, *64*	3	17	____
No Number	Similar to X-264-6, 8 pages, *64*		NRS	____
No Number	Similar to X-264-6, black binding, *64*		NRS	____
564-11	Dealer Catalog, *64*	2	8	____

1965

		Good	Exc	Cond/$
X165-12	Dealer Catalog, *65*	6	13	____
X165-12REV	Revised Dealer Catalog, *65*	6	13	____
X365-10	Consumer Folder, *65*	1.50	6	____
T465-5REV	Dealer Folder, *65*	0.85	2.50	____

1966

		Good	Exc	Cond/$
T-166-6	Dealer Catalog, *66*	4	9	____
T166-7	Gilbert Action Toys, *66*	6	32	____
X-466-1	Consumer Catalog, *66*	3	14	____
M6788	All Aboard instructions, *66*	3	8	____

1967*

		Good	Exc	Cond/$
No number	Four-page Folder, *67*	0.85	4	____

*Gilbert train production ended in 1966; however, an American Flyer Industries Folder was released for 1967.

ABBREVIATIONS
Pocket Guide Descriptions

AC	alternating current	**pass.**	passenger
bldgs.	buildings	**PB**	Alco diesel locomotive
B/W	bay window		w/o cab
comb.	combination	**PM**	Pike Master
Cond	condition	**ptd.**	painted
DC	direct current	**QE**	questionable existence
FP	diesel locomotive	**RC**	remote control
gen.	generator	**REV**	revised
GP	diesel locomotive	**RH**	right hand
Jct.	junction	**s-i-b**	smoke in boiler
KC	knuckle couplers	**s-i-t**	smoke in tender
lett.	lettering	**sta.**	station
LH	left hand	**S/W**	square window
(mv)	many variations	**u**	uncataloged
oper.	operating	**Wash.**	Washington
PA	Alco diesel locomotive w/cab	**West.**	Western

Railroad Name Abbreviations

AF (AFL)	American Flyer (Lines)	**LV**	Lehigh Valley
ART Co.	American Refrigerator Transit Co.	**MEC**	Maine Central
		MKT	Missouri-Kansas-Texas
ATSF	Atchison, Topeka and Santa Fe	**MP (MoPac)**	Missouri Pacific
		MR	Milwaukee Road
B&A	Boston and Albany	**M&StL**	Minneapolis and St. Louis
BAR	Bangor and Aroostook Railroad	**NASG**	National Association of S-Gaugers
BM	Boston and Maine		
BN	Burlington Northern	**NH**	New Haven
B&O	Baltimore and Ohio	**NKP**	Nickel Plate Road
C of G	Central of Georgia	**NP**	Northern Pacific
CB&Q	Chicago, Burlington and Quincy	**NW**	North Western
		N&W	Norfolk and Western
CMStP&P	Chicago, Milwaukee, St. Paul and Pacific	**NYC**	New York Central
		NYNH&H	New York, New Haven and Hartford
CN	Canadian National		
CNJ	Central of New Jersey	**P&LE**	Pittsburgh and Lake Erie
CNW	Chicago North Western		
C&NWRY	Chicago and North Western Railway	**PC**	Penn Central
		PRR	Pennsylvania Railroad
C&O	Chesapeake and Ohio	**REA**	Railway Express Agency
CP	Canadian Pacific	**RL**	Reading Lines
CRP	Central Railroad of Pennsylvania	**RUT**	Rutland
		SF	Santa Fe
D&H	Delaware and Hudson	**SP**	Southern Pacific
DRG	Denver and Rio Grande	**T&P**	Texas and Pacific
D&RGW	Denver and Rio Grande Western	**TCA**	Train Collectors Association
		TTOS	Toy Train Operating Society
DT&I	Detroit, Toledo, and Ironton		
GAEX	General American Express	**UFGE**	United Fruit Growers Express
		UP	Union Pacific
GM	General Motors	**USAF**	United States Air Force
GM&O	Gulf, Mobile and Ohio	**USM**	United States Marines
GN	Great Northern	**VC**	Vermont Central
HARR	Historic American Railroad	**WC**	Wisconsin Central
		WM	Western Maryland
IC	Illinois Central	**WP**	Western Pacific
L&N	Louisville and Nashville	**WSX**	White's Discount Centers
LNE	Lehigh New England		

NOTES